T0228010

PRAISE FOR

BREAKING BOTS AND JASON MARS

"Jason is a true vanguard in the lineage and development of AI, especially for what counts—the human element. As technology commoditizes the true intellectual property for AI is natural language, distinguishing AI from bots and machine learning, and accretive value-add applications of the non-technology technology. Jason's approach and success in software, building a paradigm-shifting organization, and contribution to the science of AI will continue to be groundbreaking. The application of AI in the field of human resources and its possibilities are nothing short of staggering."

—**Ryan Tweedie, CIO HR and global managing director, Accenture; former managing partner and practice leader, HR Tech, EY; former CEO, Sapien Software**

"Breaking Bots *is like two books in one! It starts off as a transparent view into the nontraditional journey of Jason Mars and his pursuit of ideas that change the world one conversation at a time. It's also a clear narrative outlining how to push this important technology past its limits with a glimpse into how far we must still go to bring bots up to speed with the sci-fi ideas that inspired their initial creation."*

—**Darrius Jones, chief strategy and marketing officer, Poly**

"Breaking Bots *is an amazing success story well worth the read. It reminds us that the mission of effectively delivering disruptive technology to the world has to begin with the passion to change the world. Jason takes us on a journey that captivatingly documents his purpose-driven formula for success as a leader, inventor, and visionary. I am forever inspired by* Breaking Bots!"

—Eldon Marks, founder and CEO, V75 Inc.

"*This is a story about defying expectation; it's about how Jason, at every step of his life, defies society's expectations and 'being twice as good,' from his upbringing to his professional career as a professor, and as an entrepreneur and a leader in the AI revolution. It is an absolute joy to read and the chapters are brimming with shards of wisdom and insights on the past, present, and future of AI.*"

—Dr. Yiping Kang, head of product, Clinc

"Breaking Bots *provides practical real-world insights into the challenges of deploying technology in today's highly complex world. Bringing new technology to bear is harder than ever with all the noise in society, and Jason's story provides an eye-opening first-person view into the realities of battling large enterprise incumbents using cutting edge research.*"

—Brian Yang, former SVP of conversational AI, Wells Fargo Bank

BREAKING BOTS

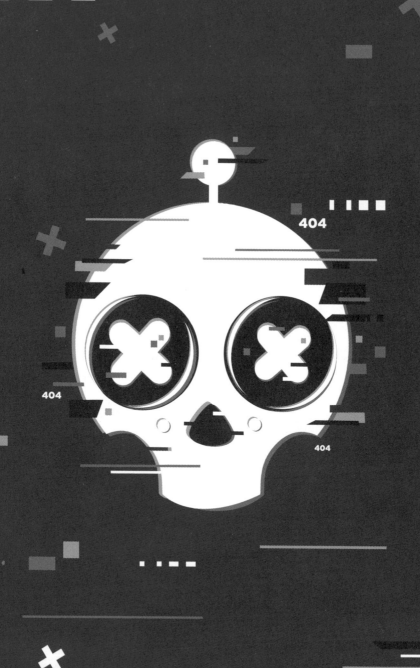

BREA

KING

BOTS

root -]$ author -n "Dr. Jason Mars"
root -]$ title -i "Breaking Bots"
Permission granted. Inventing a new
voice in the AI revolution.

ForbesBooks

Copyright © 2021 by Dr. Jason Mars.

All rights reserved. No part of this book may be used or reproduced in any manner whatsoever without prior written consent of the author, except as provided by the United States of America copyright law.

Published by ForbesBooks, Charleston, South Carolina.
Member of Advantage Media Group.

ForbesBooks is a registered trademark, and the ForbesBooks colophon is a trademark of Forbes Media, LLC.

Printed in the United States of America.

10 9 8 7 6 5 4 3 2 1

ISBN: 978-1-94663-339-2
LCCN: 2020924337

Cover and Layout design by David Taylor.

This custom publication is intended to provide accurate information and the opinions of the author in regard to the subject matter covered. It is sold with the understanding that the publisher, Advantage|ForbesBooks, is not engaged in rendering legal, financial, or professional services of any kind. If legal advice or other expert assistance is required, the reader is advised to seek the services of a competent professional.

 Advantage Media Group is proud to be a part of the Tree Neutral® program. Tree Neutral offsets the number of trees consumed in the production and printing of this book by taking proactive steps such as planting trees in direct proportion to the number of trees used to print books. To learn more about Tree Neutral, please visit **www.treeneutral.com**.

Since 1917, Forbes has remained steadfast in its mission to serve as the defining voice of entrepreneurial capitalism. ForbesBooks, launched in 2016 through a partnership with Advantage Media Group, furthers that aim by helping business and thought leaders bring their stories, passion, and knowledge to the forefront in custom books. Opinions expressed by ForbesBooks authors are their own. To be considered for publication, please visit **www.forbesbooks.com**.

To Lingjia, Xayden, Skyler, Joan, Junior, Jevan, Christian,
and all the champions in my life.

CONTENTS

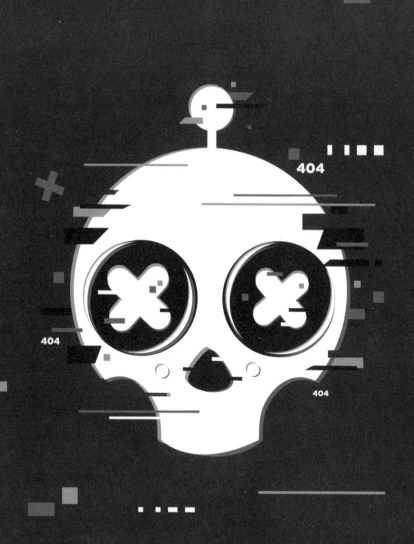

AI: A HUMAN REVOLUTION

Before humans discovered fire, we were basically indistinguishable from animals. Then, somewhere between 1.7 and 2 million years ago, we harnessed the power of fire. That achievement catapulted us beyond a state of animalism. It was arguably the first invention and technology we developed and used—to cook, to stay warm, to defend ourselves—that made us special.

By around 600 BC, we discovered electricity, and by 1800, we were sorting out how to utilize it. From then, the rate of transformational innovation increased dramatically. By 1946, we invented the first computer. Just thirty-seven years later, we invented the internet. Now, we have the ability to communicate with anyone on the planet, and we're replicating our intelligence into computers. After all, once we'd harnessed fire and electricity, it only made sense that we'd eventually want to mobilize our own intelligence as a force.

Artificial intelligence represents the ability to replicate the essence of what makes us humans interesting—which, I would say, is our intelligence. We have a tendency to claim it's this that separates

1

us from the rest of the natural world, and who's to say we're wrong? It's a massive, special, weird anomaly in the universe that we have the ability to work toward duplicating the true essence of our greatness in inanimate atoms.

Artificial intelligence represents the ability to replicate the essence of what makes us humans interesting.

We have this romantic sci-fi notion that we can take our consciousness and put it into machines. It seems far off, unreasonable even. But think back to October 13, 1966, before there were personal computers. NBC aired episode six of the very first season of *Star Trek* that day. For the first time, a Starfleet officer, Captain James T. Kirk, turns to a console on the USS *Enterprise* and says, "Computer, start." The computer listens. As the humans in the room speak to it, the computer speaks back, answering questions, responding to statements, delivering information.

And with that, a deep desire in the human subconscious became manifest: to communicate with our technology the same way we communicate with each other—through conversation. This desire represents a profound anthropological need of humans that isn't confined only to technology. We humans tend to anthropomorphize and personify anything and everything, from the teddy bears in the Care Bears, to the banana in "It's Peanut Butter Jelly Time," and even what we don't understand in a "God" (don't fret, I'm not referring to your God). We name our technological devices, we feel a fondness for our Roombas, and we talk to our computers even when they can't respond like the one on the *Enterprise* could. Human beings are a social species. We didn't evolve to type or use a mouse; we evolved to have conversations, including with our technology. We want the

USS *Enterprise* shipboard computer, J.A.R.V.I.S. from *Iron Man*, the interface from *Her*.

This natural inclination means conversational AI has long been an area of curiosity for academics. Since the 1960s, we've been studying and tinkering. People and companies have experimented with various approaches to the same problem: How can we create interfaces with technology that use voice, conversation, and, most precisely, natural language?

Three objectives are driving technology: reducing complexity, increasing convenience, and increasing delight in our lives. These drivers fuel the nearly irrational amounts of human effort and ingenuity that are required to invent. Conversational AI and AI in general are collectively our next fire, light bulb, or internet. This transformation has been our destiny since we were contemplating it in the 1960s. Thank you, Apple, Google, and Amazon, for whetting our appetite with Siri, Google Home, and Alexa. But now we're ready for what's next. There's a massive gap between the AI experiences people are using today and what our imagination necessitates.

Right now, though, we're at a bottleneck: the technology issue. Because technology is the bottleneck, it's a fascinating moment to be a scientist. Right now, it is up to us to realize the future. It's not the time of the merchants or engineers; it's the time of the scientists. I argue the oil of scientific underpinnings to create phenomenal AI is present; it needs only to be tapped.

That's why I want to share my story and the story of the company I started: Clinc. We've found ourselves at the heart of the AI revolution, and our journey has allowed me to experience where AI has been, where AI is now, and where it can go. I want you to be a part of that journey—a journey that started in a very unlikely place.

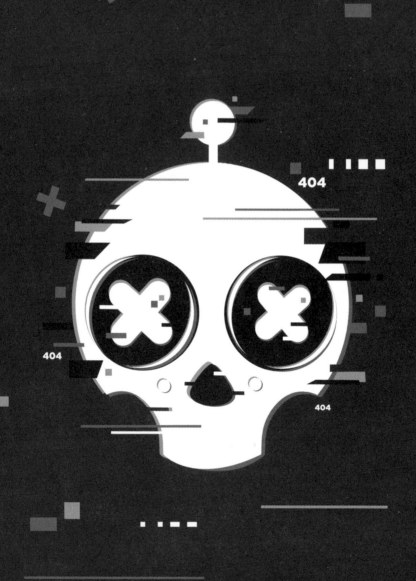

CHAPTER 1

AN UNLIKELY STORY

THE BLACK SHEEP

It's surprising that I've ended up where I am now.

My parents are from a small country in South America called Guyana, population 750,000. My mom is from a wealthier, successful family in the region; my dad, on the other hand, was from one of the poorest rural environments imaginable. He grew up in a mud house with unfavorable education prospects and barely enough food to get by. In that community, there was virtually no economy. The concept of a steady job basically didn't exist, and the idea of going to school, especially higher education, wasn't on the radar. The fact that my dad clawed himself out of this environment makes him an extraordinary case even in his own family. Most of my cousins on that side still live a lifestyle similar to my dad's lifestyle as a child.

My dad's path out started with a moment of inspired resolve that came from his neighbors' cruelty. Next door to the hut my dad grew up in was a family who lived in a house that was actually recognizable as a house. It was dilapidated and falling apart; it was not something you would call nice by any stretch of the imagination—but it was a *house*.

One night, during a terrible thunderstorm, my dad's mud house began to leak heavily while he, his mother, and his siblings desperately tried to buttress the hut's structure and keep the rain out. My dad glanced over to the neighbors' house and found them on their sheltered porch laughing hysterically at the spectacle. At that moment, one of humiliation and despair, my dad said to himself, "I'm getting the hell out of this mud hut. I'm going to live in a house. Those neighbors will see that I can live better than them."

Sometime after that night, during a visit to a doctor's office, my dad was admiring the sturdy and well-put-together office. He asked the doctor, "How did you get all of these nice things?"

The doctor looked at him discerningly and said one word: "Education."

"All right," my dad said, deciding. "Education. That's how I'm going to make it out of here."

And that's what he did. He focused on and excelled at his studies with a drive that was unmatched in his community. He got educated, got out, and became a professor of political science. He met my mother while teaching (she was actually his student at the time, but that story is for another day), and they married soon after. They had my brother during a sabbatical in California and me while they were living, studying, and teaching at the University of the West Indies in Jamaica. When I was eight, we all moved to Michigan, where both my parents joined the faculty at Wayne State University.

So, I grew up with two professor parents. It sounds like a recipe for success, but it wasn't that straightforward. Though they couldn't be prouder of me today and often brag to their friends about my accomplishments, I bet deep down it's a massive shock to my parents that I've reached this level of success.

While my older brother was (and is) a genius, I was often viewed as the black sheep of the family. I was a troublemaker, a rebel, a bad boy who refused to follow directions. As a later medical diagnosis would confirm, my rowdiness, unpredictability, and hyperactivity had a name: ADHD.

In the 1990s, the term *ADHD* was in vogue to describe any child who was not subdued and well behaved. My brother, on the other hand, earned an above-average score in eighth grade on the SAT, a college aptitude test typically taken at the end of high school. Regarded as a young black genius, he received a full scholarship to Cranbrook Schools, the poshest private school for the rich and talented in the region. Serving grades K–12 at a cost of $35,000 a year and with a $217 million endowment (more than many colleges), it was the school that senator and former presidential candidate Mitt Romney attended.

My high school was Southfield High. It ranked 13,345 out of the 17,792 high schools in the US and was predominantly black. Needless to say, the majority of the Southfield High graduates did not attend elite universities.

It's important to note that the disparity in school quality wasn't due to favoritism for my brother or neglect of my future. The reason was simple: we were poor. My brother's talents earned him a spot in an elite school, and I went to the best public school I could go to legally within the confines of my school district. My parents tried to compensate with their guidance at home, but that's difficult to do. Instead of studying and engaging in scholarly endeavors, I was obsessively focused on my own projects and interests. As far as my parents could see at the time, I was not on the same path my brother was on. They were praying that I wasn't going to follow the wrong crowd and get into trouble. That might be an unfair simplification, but it's pretty close to the truth.

Being professors, my parents were sticklers for education. But school didn't capture my interest. I was into playing video games. Then, when I was thirteen or fourteen, I learned there were programs out there that would let you edit those games. There was an entire "modding" (short for *modification*) scene dedicated to this. You could take *Doom* and actually change how it worked by giving yourself the ability to jump four times higher. You could make the weapons ten times more powerful so that when you shot an enemy, they would explode into little "giblets."

The fact that I could alter the rules of how the game worked blew my mind. "I've got to double down on this," I thought. So, I did. I learned that the way people create video games was something called *programming* or *coding*—and that's how this journey started.

I taught myself everything about it that I could, including the C++ programming language so I could write video games. Out of necessity, I also taught myself how to fix old, broken-down computers. Money was tight, and if I had a crappy, burned-out hard drive, I had to learn how to make it function.

Of course, all this newfound knowledge also led me into the exhilarating world of computer hacking.

THE HACKER

In the early days of the internet, there was a major hacking phreacking warez scene—*warez* meaning pirated software, super old school. People would set up their own little servers called bulletin board services, or BBSs, and one of the things you could find were programs that could generate legitimate credit card numbers.

I came across this when I was twelve or thirteen. I thought it was interesting, so I tinkered with these programs and generated a bunch of credit card numbers. I never did anything with the numbers; I just explored how these programs worked.

Back then, the most popular way to get the internet was to subscribe to a service like AOL. I signed up for a free trial with a competing service called CompuServe, which in my opinion was better than AOL. After the free trial, it would be forty dollars a month.

When the trial was about to run out, I asked my mom if we could continue the subscription.

"You're too young for that nonsense," she said.

I was livid—and desperate. In anger and rebellion, I thought, "I've never actually tried one of these credit card numbers. Maybe I can extend the trial by putting one in." I went to one of the programs, hit the "Generate" button, and put the number generated into the form for CompuServe. I had no idea if it would actually work.

Until I hit "Submit."

It worked.

The first emotion I felt was "Sweet!" immediately followed by complete and utter panic.

I realized I had broken a law, and I was terrified. Around that time, it was a common occurrence for FBI SWAT teams to show up at a hacker's house, kick in the door, raid the house, and arrest the hacker. You'd see it all the time in newspapers: a skinny teenager led out of a suburban house in handcuffs, surrounded by a SWAT team, his parents in the doorway looking horrified. Right after hitting "Submit," I knew that could be me.

I immediately deactivated the account and hid my laptop in a closet. For three days, I was completely panicked, waiting for our door to be kicked down.

Fortunately, they never came. Never again would I do such a thing; I spooked myself into oblivion.

But it didn't mean I was done with computer mischief. I became an expert on computer viruses. In fact, I got suspended once for getting viruses on our school computers. It was at a middle school in Wisconsin where I went temporarily while my mom was doing a short stint as a professor at the University of Wisconsin and my dad was teaching in Detroit. The middle school had computers. They were old, slow, outdated machines, but they had internet. The school's computer lab was my only access to internet at the time, and that's where I could research "virii" (the cool hacker name for viruses). My browsing history was filled with my activity in the virii scene.

I started researching viruses to find ones I thought were really cool, and I downloaded them to a floppy disk for my collection. I was particularly fascinated with polymorphic viruses—*polymorphic* meaning the virus changes itself automatically over time, making it difficult to detect with a virus scan. There was one virus in particular that I believe was called "neurokilla." This was the one I inadvertently unleashed on the school. It was silent and stealthy, and it was claimed to randomly kill computers in an irreparable way in a certain span of time after it was deployed. I dug deeper.

Through my research, I learned it would interfere with the computer's boot sequence by obliterating the MBR, the master boot record. If you corrupt the MBR on older machines, the computer won't boot because it won't recognize the disk. Sure, it's possible to rescue such systems—but you'd need someone more sophisticated than the middle school IT guy.

All it took for a computer to contract this deadly virus was an infected floppy disk. Stick it in, boot the machine, and the computer would be infected—and nobody would know for another week or two until the computer suddenly up and died. Maybe it was an accident, maybe curiosity, but after I spent a day in the lab tinkering with viruses, an epidemic began.

One computer down. Two computers down. Five computers down. Two weeks later, every single computer was down. They tried to fix them, but of course they couldn't. So guess what the administration did? They bought all new Pentiums for the lab to replace the 486s that died a tragic death by neurokilla. At the time I felt like a vigilante hero who, though unintentionally, brought some good to all the kids at the school.

It didn't go off completely without a hitch. In the course of my tinkering, I accidentally infected my own computer at home with the same virus. Like the school computers, it appeared pretty much unfixable. Unfortunately, I didn't have the money for a new hard drive, and I couldn't tell my mom that I busted my computer. I had no choice but to fix it myself, and it was quite an ordeal. I didn't sleep for three days, trying to do it. I learned all about an MBR and how it works. I had to find

> **The amount of computer science I learned restoring my computer from my own virus was truly astronomical.**

these gnarly tools that let you scrub your hard drive, block by block, so I could reflash it from scratch. The amount of computer science I learned restoring my computer from my own virus was truly astronomical for a middle schooler.

Of course, looking back, all of this was technically vandalism.

I was a crazy and stupid kid, and it was a crazy and stupid idea to play with computer viruses on public property. It wasn't until a full semester after this inadvertent activism that I was finally outed. I had an argument with one of my few friends at the school about which Power Ranger was superior to the others (clearly the black ranger), and he ratted me out.

"We're considering expulsion," the principal told my mortified parents. "This is vandalism. We have his browsing history as evidence." The principal showed them my browsing history, which plainly tracked my research into the virus.

My mom pleaded with the school, and they agreed to suspend me for two days. After that year, we returned to Southfield, Michigan, for my mom's new job at University of Michigan-Flint.

THE LONER

That was my life growing up: stressing out my parents, getting into computer mischief, pulling crazy stunts, playing and making video games, and not focusing on my academics. As a black nerd, I didn't adjust well to high school in the Detroit metropolitan area. I was interested in learning but not in what they were teaching me. All I wanted to do was code. On my own I studied math for 3D graphics and how to build 3D graphics engines from scratch, pixel by pixel. I spent class time reading my book on college-level analytic geometry, refusing to pay attention to what was being taught. Rarely did I do homework. I had no respect for my teachers, because I felt like I was so far ahead of them. And they just saw me as a peculiar kid.

My disconnect was compounded by the fact that my high school did not set me up for success. I learned years later that it was in the bottom-third percentile of high schools in the country. It was also

90 percent black. We were not encouraged to pursue our dreams or attend college. A couple of neighborhoods over, in the wealthy white area, there was a different narrative. Kids there were encouraged to continue their education at the highest levels beyond high school. They were told it was their right, their future, the story they could expect to live.

In our school, we were repeatedly told that our lone path to any success was likely vocational school. I recall one day when all seniors had to attend a special session about a program in which we could apply with the local power company to climb poles and repair lines for a living. This was the type of blue-collar position that we were supposed to aim for, and the program is why a disproportionate number of black students follow such a path. There is nothing wrong with working on power lines, but when it is one of only a few opportunities presented to students, there is little chance they will ever discover and maximize their potential. They stay in that socioeconomic bracket and send their kids to the same poor school, and the cycle continues. It's systemic. And, of course, it's a system that extends far beyond schools today. It reaches back to the origins of the black experience post–Civil War and throughout all areas of society.

The only reason I didn't end up in that cycle is because of the stringent guidance my parents provided me and the focus they put on continuing my education. While my school didn't really care, my parents brainwashed me on the importance of education.

That didn't stop me from constantly complaining to them about high school. "I'm all alone!" I insisted. "There aren't even any programming classes in my school. Can't I just drop out? I'm not learning anything!"

Of course, dropping out was heresy to my mom. "Jason, if you do anything like that, I will destroy you," my mom said. "You have to stay in high school because you have to go to college."

"Mom, I'm literally wasting my time!" I exclaimed. "I go there every day and waste my time, and then I come home and spend all night actually doing something real and cool. Why do I have to do this?" I was convinced that there was no way to learn but on my own. A quote I rediscovered on my programming website from when I was fifteen years old really shows my state of mind at the time: "I have asked a lot of people to help me with this project, but all I hear is 'no.' So I just want to say to all those people that didn't believe me: SEE, I'LL DO IT, AND ALL BY MYSELF. SO HA."

"I promise you, Jason," my mom said, "college will be completely different. It's a wonderful place where you can pursue your passion, where you'll find your people."

I bought it. My parents convinced me that when I got to college, I'd find I wasn't alone in the world. That meant something to a weird kid like me. Because that's what I was: a weird, weird kid, an outcast living not even on cloud nine—I was somewhere out on cloud seventeen. The popular kids in high school were smoking marijuana, having sex, playing sports. I didn't do any of that. While the cool kids all showed off their new clothes and shoes, I wore the same ripped pants and grubby T-shirts every day. I didn't know how to socialize. I didn't have any friends. I was, to put it mildly, not popular. And I wondered, "Where are the other Jasons?" I didn't have a community. My parents convinced me that in college I would.

But that was not the case.

When I got to the University of Pittsburgh, the first thing I did was look for my people. I found all the kids in my freshman class who were coders—and I was shocked by how far below my capability they were. I had written entire programming languages, programming compilers, and 3D game engines from scratch in C++ while still in high school. They were writing toy applications in Visual Basic. The capability gap was too large. They didn't know what the hell I was talking about. I was still alone.

The education didn't live up to the hype either, at least not at first. I skipped about half my programming lectures for the first two years of computer science classes, just coming in for the tests—for which I didn't bother to study. I got Bs and B-minuses in every class. It wasn't until I started going to upper-level classes that I actually began learning new things and becoming engaged.

And then, something happened. Or I should say, *someone* happened.

It was one day in my sophomore year. I went to the office of my favorite lecturer and showed off all my cool pet projects, hoping he'd appreciate them. With what I can describe only as complete bewilderment on his face, he immediately referred me to a professor of research. I booked the meeting and went to her office.

"Jason, I'm Professor Mary Lou Soffa," she said. Before she could continue her introduction, I went nuts showing her all my cool stuff.

"You need to join my research group," she said. Somehow, Professor Soffa saw my potential. She didn't ask about my grades or background, yet she was convinced I would make important contributions to her lab. So I started to spend my summers with her research group and entered the land of research academia.

It was there I discovered this world where you get to tinker, discover problems, conjure solutions, and apply every ounce of your creativity toward doing something cool. It's a world where you get to invent things and then have society reward you for them at the highest level. I had finally found my niche. Within the institutional academic framework, I could do all the cool stuff I'd always wanted to do. I could be an inventor and write papers about my inventions, which would give me the freedom to travel the world and talk about my work. I could forever pursue whatever I wanted to work on, as long as it was considered interesting.

So, I decided to go the PhD route, doing only research that mattered, research that I wanted to do, research that would change the world of technology.

THE FIVE-POUND WEIGHT

That was all great, but postcollege is also where my experience as a black person got more interesting. When I was working at Google, where I interned five different times over the summers, people assumed I was a cook. I remember walking down the hall one day talking to someone, and it came up that I was an engineer. "Dude," the person I was talking to said, "I didn't realize you were an engineer! I thought you worked in the kitchen!" In the moment, it didn't really bother me, but the next time I walked down that hall, I suddenly realized, "Shit, most of these people probably think I'm a cook."

That's the five-pound weight I carry with me all the time: the knowledge that most people probably think I'm the cook or the janitor or the maintenance guy, not an engineer, not a professor, not a CEO. How do I compensate for that? How do I look more like an engineer, a professor, a CEO? That's what privilege is: not having to think about that, not having to carry that five pounds.

Of course, this can be true for everyone who doesn't "look the part." Someone with epic tats and earlobe stretching and bright-green hair might have the same problem. It's just unfortunate, because I have no say about being black. I didn't have to get tattoos or dye my hair to achieve that level of baggage.

But even with the advantage of being a man, I always need to lift up that five-pound weight of being black before people stop questioning whether I'm an engineer. When I talk to investors, I see a difference in the way they engage with me based on their first impression and the way they engage with me ten seconds after I start talking and they learn my background. It actually feels good, because I totally obliterate the first impression they formed based on what I look like.

However, I also go through the world knowing sometimes you don't get a chance to obliterate that first impression. You don't get to start talking to people. Sometimes, all someone sees is a black guy. And I'll tell you where it gets hard: it's the psychology of knowing that you're black. When I was at Google, I wouldn't see any other black people in the engineering group. And I would forget that I was black—until someone assumed I was a cook and was surprised to learn I was actually an engineer. Even today, I rarely see any black people on a day-to-day basis, and I forget that I'm black. I don't have a lot of opportunities to feel my blackness. It's crazy.

But no one else forgets I'm black, so I carry this reality with me all the time. I know I'll be considered a little bit less if I don't get the chance to demonstrate that I'm just as good or better. It's been conditioned into me hardcore since I got out of college. When I became a professor, I knew without a question I had to have a better record than every other faculty member in the department. I had to mitigate the expectations people had based on my blackness by being twice as good. I had to have the audacity to be better than everyone's expectations—and that audacity has guided my journey and allowed me to believe I can use my work to change the world.

CHAPTER 2

TIME TO CHANGE THE WORLD

LINGJIA

When Professor Soffa was hired by the University of Virginia, I went with her and joined her lab there. Almost as soon as I arrived, I met Lingjia Tang, the woman who would become my partner, in work and in life.

When I met Lingjia, she was struggling. She was working with an advisor who was not doing top work and for whom all his other students were struggling at the time. When we started dating, I encouraged her to join my research lab and work with my advisor instead. She did, and we embarked on a journey of intense work together, staying up all night doing research and writing papers, loving every moment of it.

We were—and are—a perfect match, because while we are both

ambitious, we are ambitious for different reasons. I want to change the world. Lingjia wants to be the best at whatever she does. She loves to kick ass and feel that rush of domination. I want to see my work move mountains for the greater good. It's a great synergy.

I want to see my work move mountains for the greater good.

At UVA, we did extraordinary work together, publishing a slew of top-notch papers and changing the landscape of publications at UVA for our area of study. Then we became professors together at the University of California San Diego and stayed for a year before we were both recognized and poached by the University of Michigan, which made us an offer we couldn't refuse.

The computer science department and faculty at Michigan were our idols when we were PhD students. We read and admired their research and were very motivated by the fact that the department had, and still has, an unusual concentration of computer science superstars. So, when we got the offer, we immediately said, "Hell, yeah, we're going to Michigan!" To be in that environment, to survive and thrive among those legends, was a challenge we had to accept.

Lingjia and I are still professors at Michigan, and in our time here, we've broken a number of records with regard to research productivity in the most prestigious venues in our field. In order to earn tenure at a school like Michigan, you have to publish roughly six top-tier papers, among other achievements. I've published thirty-plus top-tier papers, putting me in well-respected Hall of Fame listings while still pretenure at the same time full professors at other prestigious schools were being inducted. It didn't take long for our worldly vision to feel constrained within the confines of academia, so we branched out—launching our own company to bring true innovation and impact to the masses.

"HEAR YOU; NO!"

Lingjia and I became professors for one reason: we thought it was the perfect platform to change the world with technology. That's what sent us on a research trajectory in 2013 that would eventually become Clinc in 2015. The mission of our lab—a talented research group of two professors, Lingjia, me, and fourteen PhD students—was to envision what the landscape of computing would look like ten years from today and focus on and solve a problem that would change that landscape.

Circa 2013, it was clear to us that if we wanted to focus our energy on solving the relevant problems and barriers in the next generation of technology, there was only one place to look: artificial intelligence. That would be the next big technological leap forward. There was a deep craving for artificial intelligence applications in the market. So, while the rest of our community at the time considered web search engines and social networks the things to study, we were among the first systems labs to look at artificial intelligence from an academic perspective, researching where AI would be in a decade.

Along that journey, we created a research project we called Sirius.[1] We wanted to build a kind of conversational AI platform that utilized the technologies of the future. We wanted to build it end to end, and we wanted it to be big, so we studied what would happen to the world if we made it to scale.

---

1   Johann Hauswald et al, "Sirius: An open end-to-end voice and vision personal assistant and its implications for future warehouse scale computers," *Proceedings of the Twentieth International Conference on Architectural Support for Programming Languages and Operating Systems*, 2015, 223–238.

In 2013, when we were working on Sirius, there was no deep AI on the critical path web search queries. That would quickly change by 2015 with the Google RankBrain project, which started to do embeddings in search queries.[2] Back then, the general approach to web search was something called a reverse index, which can be (perhaps unfairly) simplified as sophisticated keyword matching. Every query put into a web search engine had to do that work.

So we said, "Let's imagine that in the next ten years, every query needs to interact with AI—and perhaps AI that is conversational." If we had a world where every query was routed to a virtual system and where those queries were delivered conversationally instead of being typed in, what would have to happen from a system-stacked cross-layer perspective? What do the models look like? What has to happen in the application? What must occur in the infrastructure to support that computation?

We discovered something phenomenal: at the time, it would take about thirty-two nuclear power plants' worth of energy to support web search. In order to support the next generation of this kind of AI technology, the computations would have to be scaled by a factor of 168 times.

That would be completely unsustainable—which led us to our next task. We worked on how to make adjustments across the entire stack, from application to models to computer infrastructure, in order to mitigate that 168-times scale. And we arrived at a solution framework that could bring it down to a factor of sixteen.

That was the first step in Sirius: creating a virtual system that represented what would happen in ten years. Through that work, we

2   Cade Metz, "AI Is Transforming Google Search. The Rest of the Web Is Next," *Wired*, February 4, 2106, https://www.wired.com/2016/02/ai-is-changing-the-technology-behind-google-searches/.

gained incredible amounts of expertise in the technologies available and the technologies that were necessary to represent the future of conversational AI. Then, we took the prototypes we had built in that research work and made an end-to-end system available to the world, a system we called Sirius. From that point we'd proceed to publish fifteen more top-tier papers digging deep into the nuances of systems and AI for the future, building a deep expertise and insight in our lab that would become indispensable with the coming endeavor to impact the world.

The launch of Sirius itself had a massive impact. When we open-sourced Sirius, all sorts of companies started using it. It was all going great—until we got a letter from Apple.

Now, you may have noticed something about the name *Sirius*: it sounds a lot like Siri. And yeah, that's part of the inspiration for the name. But Sirius is also named after the so-called Dog Star. *Sirius* is a word and a name in its own right, not inherently connected to Siri.

The problem was that we were too successful. So Apple's legal team sent us a note saying, "You're infringing on our trademark. Your system is too popular, and it's starting to hurt our ability to contain our brand. So you have to change the name."

I had only one response: "Hear you, and no."

We weren't messing in Apple's land. Our research lab isn't a company. Sirius was an academic project that we were making available to anyone who wanted it, in the spirit of impacting the world by letting more folks discover what needs to happen for the future progress of AI. I'm not a lawyer, but it was my understanding that when you're in the academic sphere, you don't have the same legal requirement for trademarks and such. As an academic project, you're protected. I even did some research and found some cases that set this precedent.

I wanted to fight. I was *ready* to fight.

But it wasn't up to me. The university got to make that decision. And the first thing the university said to me was, and I paraphrase: "Holy shit, Jason. This is Apple. We can't fight Apple. Just imagine the resources needed to go up against Apple. Also, they have really good lawyers. We probably won't win that fight. So the easiest thing is for you to just change the name. Yep. That's what we want you to do. Just change the name."

My response? The same as last time: "Hear you; no. I'm not changing the name. Just send a response letter saying this is an academic project. There's no lawsuit yet; just fight the lawyers a little bit and see if they back off. It's just a discussion at this point. So, discuss."

"Look, Jason," the university said, "we really think you should change the name. We looked at it and Apple may have a case, and if we try to fight it, it'll cost us millions of dollars. We don't have the budget for that."

Meanwhile, the department chair at the time was wondering what this ruckus was all about. I said to him, "You can't tell me that we don't have the cojones to try to make a case and just see how they respond."

"You know, you're right," he said. "We need to at least try. We don't necessarily have to engage in a lawsuit, but let's try to make the case."

So the university's lawyers tried to make the case. Months went by, and Apple was still saying, "Change the name." Now, they weren't threatening to sue at this point, so I felt like we were making progress. But the university's lawyers didn't want to bear the risk. Eventually, they'd had enough and tapped out. "We've decided to move ahead with a process that removes the university as the culpable party, and you will be directly culpable," they stated in an email to me. Or, in other words, you have to defend this yourself, and if you lose, they're coming after you personally. They made it so I was an independent entity, no longer protected by the university.

My response was short and to the point:

"You know what?" I said. "There are a lot of good names out there. I should just change the name."

And so we changed the project's name to Lucida, which is the word for the brightest star in a constellation.

THE BIRTH OF CLINC

When we launched Sirius/Lucida, we received an enormous amount of interest. We published award-winning papers and got a lot of press for our work, which is relatively rare for professors' research in our area. We were written up in *Wired* magazine, and it wasn't long before random people and enterprises across the world were reaching out to us. General Electric got in touch, saying, "We want to use this so our mechanics who are working on airplanes can get hands-free information while they work." Wells Fargo wanted to understand how they could use our technology to build their own conversational AI. We even heard from an Australian police department that said, "We need conversational AI in our vehicles so our cops can talk to it instead of having to type on a laptop."

It was clear there was a void in the market for technology that worked. Even though all these big companies like Google and Apple were building conversational AI, the market was still screaming for something better. They were desperately seeking a solution to their problems. We studied this void using the expertise we'd accumulated in how to build these complicated systems, and we realized how uniquely qualified we were. That's when we said, "Dude, we've got to start a company!"

Now, at this point, Lingjia and I were pretenure. One of the most accepted and understood things about tenure is that while you are trying to achieve it, you are usually focused on hacking and optimizing metrics related to it rather than genuinely making an impact on the world. You publish X papers. You go to and serve on the PC of Y conferences. When you teach, you schmooze students with doughnuts in class around professor evaluation time to get good reviews. You do things to make sure all your colleagues love you.

One thing you do *not* do is start a company. That's for after tenure. All missions to change the world fall into this category.

But for Lingjia and me, our MO with nonsense that violates our principles has always been, "Hear you; no." It's in our DNA. It's part of our spirit. If there's a higher truth out there we want to pursue, no institutional or human inefficiency should stand in our way. That truth for us was that we are professors because we want to make a real contribution to society. That is our first-order goal.

So I said, "Let's start this company and change the world."

A lot of professors who start companies do so to make money from their research. Often, they'll select one of their students to be the CEO so they can continue to work on many other projects while reaping the profits. That didn't make sense to me. If I wanted to change the world, I was going to have to drive the company myself. I couldn't rely on anyone else to do it.

So, three years into my tenure track, I went on leave from being a professor and started Clinc. And even though that's something you typically shouldn't do pretenure, the University of Michigan cares about real impact in the world. It didn't affect my tenure case, because it was understood that while on my journey to change the world, I would accomplish significant work that the university would value. I would continue publishing compelling papers. I would make important dents in improving technology. Michigan is one of those outstanding universities that value the higher mission that universities should serve the world.

Being pretenure wasn't the only thing that made creating the company a crazy idea. There was also the fact that Lingjia and I were about to have a baby.

When we started talking about creating a company, we talked about when the right time would be to do it. We had emails coming in from people who wanted our tech. It's not like interest was going to wane, but we also didn't want to miss our shot.

"Well, you know, it'll come soon," I said. "We're having a baby, so let's figure that out and then we can start the company."

"Hear you; no," Lingjia replied. "Let's just start the company."

So we did. We launched Clinc in July 2015—just one week after our baby was born.

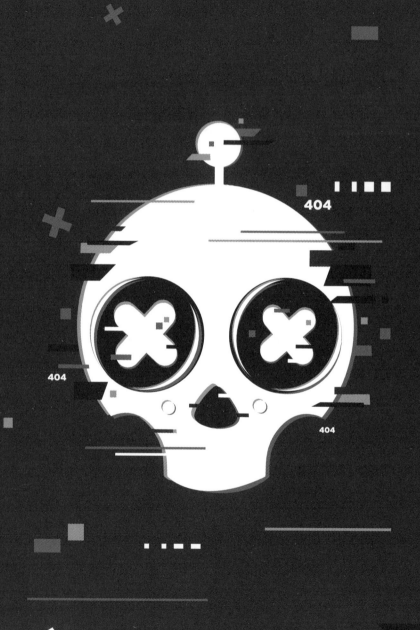

CHAPTER 3

YOUNG, SCRAPPY, AND HUNGRY

SHOW; DON'T TELL

Sirius is old tech compared to what we started working on at Clinc. When we founded Clinc, we didn't use any of what we invented for Sirius/Lucida. We wanted to create the most sophisticated conversational AI platform on the planet from the bottom up through research and invention. And over our first year, we did just that. In 2016, we unveiled Clinc's conversational AI platform to the world.

But the technology was only part of the equation. We also had to determine how to bring it to market. Should we just build this cool tech, then sell it to other start-ups so that they could build products? Or should we bring it to market ourselves? In the first few months, we were building and ideating, ideating and building. Then, we got our first seed-level tech investor. They weren't in the same tier as the top investors in the country; they were a local investment firm. But they were excited about what we were doing.

We did what's called a tranche deal, in which the investor invests in two stages. In the first stage, they give you a portion of the money in exchange for a piece of equity. In the second stage, they give you the rest of the money for more equity. Between the first and second portions, there are milestones set up that the company must accomplish in order to receive the second sum of money. However, the investor ultimately decides if they want to invest that second sum. They could choose not to and keep only the equity from the initial tranche.

The investor joined our board, which also consisted of Lingjia and me. They had created a well-thought-out plan for the company, and their aim was to provide us guidance on how to reach the milestones in that plan.

If you are familiar with companies in their nascent stages, you know that whatever plan you have needs to evolve as the company grows. Things are going to shift and change.

The plan the investors had for us was to go to market ourselves and obtain letters of intent, or LOIs. In an LOI, a company says, "I intend to buy your product when it's ready." This unsavvy practice today was somewhat common back then, and it's what our investors felt we needed to do. They didn't know anything about technology; they knew everything about sales. From their perspective, the more customers we could secure in advance, the better.

While I understood their approach, we were a small company of only about seven or eight people. Instead of working on the technology, we would all have to be out selling, including our engineers. I didn't think this plan of attack would work, and it didn't. Not only did we have nothing to show potential customers when we were out selling, since none of us were back in the lab building the technology, but the market was full of noise. There were hundreds of start-ups all offering crappy chatbots with old, inadequate technology yet claiming to have the most amazing AI in the world. And we couldn't prove that we were better than they were because we had nothing to show.

The way I saw it, we had two options: we could continue to grind it out as we were and try to squeak out the LOI quota our investor wanted so that we could secure the next chunk of cash, or we could do something much bolder.

"Forget the milestones," I told our team. "Let's be different from all the other start-ups and build something that demonstrates the future. Then we'll show it to the world."

We targeted Finovate, a top industry conference for banking and financial technology, as the place where we would demonstrate what we'd built, something irrefutably ahead of everything anyone had ever seen. But we had only eight months until the conference. We had to work hard and fast on building our technology.

As you can imagine, our investor wasn't happy about our decision. They thought we'd gone mad, and they were upset that we weren't following their plan. But I assured them it would be worth it. I was confident that once they saw the market response at Finovate, they would offer us the second part of their investment.

Yes, we were taking a huge risk. But with great risk can come significant reward—and that's what happened to us. We drove, we grinded, and we built something truly phenomenal: a next-level experience. When launch day arrived at Finovate, our presentation was off the charts. I demonstrated an experience that was light years ahead of any kind of virtual assistant imaginable—and that wasn't all. We did something people in the market never did: we provided six devices to people in the audience that they could actually use. It was such a hit that we won "Best of Show." The tech worked with strangers coming to our booth without any priming. They just talked to our AI, and in numerous languages.

And with that came the customers that our investor wanted. In fact, it was at Finovate that we landed our first big customer: one of the top banks in the US, which I'll call US-AY-AY. But as usual, we did it in a very unconventional way.

Mac Simpson, the CIO of US-AY-AY at the time, didn't want to come to our booth at first. They already had an AI solution from a company called Nuance that they had paid millions of dollars for. So, instead of waiting for him to come to our booth, I took our booth over to him. I grabbed one of our devices and a phone, and I headed his way.

"Here," I said as I handed him the phone. "This thing knows about your bank account. Ask it something."

Probably just to get me out of his hair, he appeased me by putting on the attached headphones and began to interact with it. Within seconds, his eyebrows went up.

"What's going on with my money?" he asked, and it responded.

"How much did I spend going out to dinner last week?" he asked, and it had an answer.

There was noise all around, with people talking, eating hors d'oeuvres, and wandering through the booths, but he was fully engrossed—because this thing I handed him actually worked. In that moment, we acquired him as a customer.

Letting people play with an AI product live and uncoached as we did is the riskiest thing a company can do, and it normally doesn't happen. In the AI world, most companies tell a big story but then disappoint because they don't really have what they say they have. That's what makes Clinc unique. It's why our mantra, "Show; don't tell," is one of a kind in the AI world. We're not just going to tell you about all this cool tech; we're going to show it to you. Even as we've grown, we've kept that deep care and culture of delivering on our promise. It's about keeping our word and having evidence to support our claims. I am a hardliner on making sure we can do everything we promise.

I am a hardliner on making sure we can do everything we promise.

Our academic research lab has always had a culture of truth seeking, a culture of keeping it real. You can't hand-wave or BS your way through something. You have to do top-notch research. Your idea needs to be thought out, with evidence to support whatever you're claiming.

ON OUR OWN

After Finovate, we met for dinner with some of the partners in the investment firm backing us. We were coming to the end of our first tranche, and we were out of money. Everyone in the company had been paid, but Lingjia and I had stopped paying ourselves four months earlier. Our team was running on fumes.

At our meeting, one of the partners wasted no time getting to the issue at hand.

"Jason, I need you to sell us on why we should give you this next big chunk of cash."

"You saw the journey," I replied. "You saw the vision, and you saw the product we created. I'm not going to try to sell you on anything. If you don't believe in what you saw, in what we showed you, then I don't want your money."

After all, if we took their money, they would receive a larger stake in Clinc at the low valuation of Clinc before we had achieved so much. And did we really want people who didn't believe in us owning a large chunk of our company at a crazy low price? It would have been another 15 percent of Clinc for $750,000.

There were four partners involved, and all of them had to agree. One truly believed in us and would have given us the money then and there. But the other three weren't convinced. I knew how much more valuable we were than when these guys first invested. We had demonstrated a product that was miles ahead of what anybody else had. We were getting big businesses to drop their incumbent AI platforms in order to adopt ours.

"Listen," I told the other three investors. "You're about to receive a significant chunk of our company. It's the best deal on the planet after this performance. And you don't believe in us? If you've got the vision, then prove it to us. If you don't have the vision to make the right call here, then I don't want to work with you."

They made their call: they didn't give us the second tranche.

Fortunately, we had tethered their board seat to the second tranche. So, they were off the board, and out of the company. To me, this was a relief. We had our board back, we had our company back, and we didn't have these people who didn't believe in us.

Unfortunately, though, we also didn't have any money. It was November, and we would be completely flat broke by January. In my mind, money or no money, we were still driving forward. Even if we had to lay off everybody, the other cofounders and I would work for free. We had a product that was dominating everything else out there, and we had excited and engaged potential customers. We weren't about to quit.

So we kept going—and before those three months were out, we had another investor who saw what we had and was blown away. By the end of the year we raised a $6.5 million Series A round for

20 percent of the company, a much better deal than giving away 15 percent for $750,000.

Although it all worked out in the end, saying no to that money was one of the riskiest things Clinc ever did—but it was necessary to get where we are today. If we had spent all that time selling LOIs, we never would have built the product. We never would have had something to show instead of tell.

Now, "Show; don't tell" has become one of our prime tenets. While most AI companies will tell you all about the goose that lays the golden egg and show you a slide with a goose laying a golden egg, we're the only company that shows you the live goose actually laying that golden egg. That's our principle, and we wouldn't have been able to do any of it if we hadn't said, "Hear you; no" to the investors who didn't believe in what we did.

SALES TACTIC: TELL THE TRUTH

Immediately after Mac Simpson interacted with our AI, he assigned his top lieutenant the task of bringing in Clinc. In fact, it was the same guy who had brought in Nuance. And there were still several people in the organization who were sold on Nuance, which created some difficulties for us. But the lieutenant, Damian Smith, is the kind of guy who always wants to find the next best thing.

When we had our call with Damian, he was skeptical. He's seen a thousand conversational AI companies, and they were all full of it—including Nuance. Nuance had closed the deal with US-AY-AY a year before they even built the product. They sold US-AY-AY a product that didn't exist, then built the product after the deal was done. Sounds weird, right? But that's the way most AI companies operated. This wasn't a slam dunk even though Mac was all in. We needed Damian too.

In late October 2016, we went to Money 20/20, another financial conference. Mac was there. Damian was there. Christina Nichol, another one of Mac's lieutenants, was there too. We met them in person and had a nice chat.

"Hey, Damian," Mac said. "How's it going? Are we moving forward with Clinc?"

"Well," Damian said, "I've got to talk to some people about our contract with Nuance. I want to get things lined up right ..."

Mac gave him a look that clearly said, "What are you doing? We need to move on this now!"

Damian agreed, and he started to take us more seriously. We showed him the same thing that we had shown Mac at Finovate.

"I get it," Damian said. "We're going to accelerate this."

And about a month later, we had a deal. Compared to what we make today, it wasn't much money. But it was the first money we'd gotten from a customer, and we were thrilled.

We went to the ends of the earth to make sure that US-AY-AY knew they'd made the right choice. We went on-site and did what I call "the razzle-dazzle." It's a special kind of meeting where we show people the phenomenon of what we do. This is a necessity, because when people hear about what we do, their brains link it to the thing they know, which is usually some awful chatbot experience they had. Until you see it, until we show it to you, you can't possibly understand. So, we have these "razzle-dazzle" meetings so you can experience it for yourself.

Damian's right-hand man, Macho Manning, was key in making these sessions happen. Macho would later join Clinc, but he worked with us on the US-AY-AY side for our first year there. Every time we'd go to US-AY-AY, he would orchestrate meetings to which he'd bring all the business units, all the key decision makers, and all the stakeholders, and we'd show them what we'd built for US-AY-AY.

At Clinc, we have a unique sales tactic: tell the truth. It started when we were selling ourselves to US-AY-AY, and I was really the only sales guy at the company—and I am not a sales guy. I'm an inventor and scientist. I went to these meetings without any actual sales experience or knowledge in how to sell. So I just did what I knew how to do: I made technical arguments and told the truth. The technology came from my vision, after all, so I was able to talk about it with more knowledge than any other human on earth. I knew what deep technical choices were made and why, because I was the one who made those choices.

> At Clinc, we have a unique sales tactic: tell the truth.

By this time, Damian Smith was passionate about Clinc. He moved heaven and earth to make sure the organizational complexities of US-AY-AY were mitigated to give us a clear path to earn the big contract—which we ultimately did.

US-AY-AY was our first big client—and I'll be telling more stories about how we convinced other giant companies to take a chance on our young, scrappy start-up. Today, the banks that thought we were too small, that said, "There's no way you can handle us," are coming back to us, wanting to be involved.

None of this would have happened if we hadn't been able to show, not tell. In order to show, we had to develop technology that nobody else was developing—not even the big companies with their multimillion-dollar research labs. How in the world were we able to do that?

Because Clinc has a DNA that is truly special and unique.

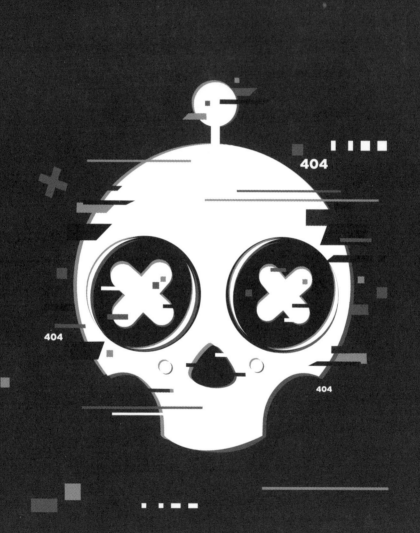

CHAPTER 4

A UNIQUE DNA—THE WHY BEHIND CLINC'S TECHNICAL SUPERIORITY

THE JUGGERNAUT TOPPLER

Most companies have research labs—Nokia Bell Labs, Microsoft Research, IBM's Thomas J Watson Research Center, Google DeepMind, Facebook Research. And they're all pouring massive sums of money into artificial intelligence.

So, if all these companies are working heavily, investing heavily, and spending billions of dollars on the same holy grail problem of conversational AI, why is it that a start-up can come in and disrupt that space? How can Clinc be toppling these juggernauts?

It's because we have a company culture and DNA that has led us to do everything differently and authentically. Lingjia and I started

Clinc with the purpose of impacting the world. That is spooled into the DNA of the company, and it's why we are successful. The truth is, from the time I was putting viruses on middle school computers, that's all I've wanted to do: change the freaking world.

Clinc is a manifestation of research and invention that was built in the lab at the University of Michigan with Lingjia and fourteen PhD students (nine of whom are the core of our company today). In this lab, we forged a perspective on how to build these systems and impact people's lives with this technology.

RESEARCH THAT MATTERS

Typically, tech companies fall into one of two categories.

First, there are companies like Cisco, made up of a bunch of businesspeople with no scientists. The group of businesspeople said, "Chatbots are trending. Let's start a chatbot company and make money. Bring up all your businesspeople, and we'll hire some smart engineers. We'll also hire a data scientist, and then we'll have the data scientist put together a team who can build what we need." The problem is that while people conflate the two all the time, data scientists are not machine-learning computer scientists, and they can't do this kind of work. But the businesspeople don't know any better.

The other type of company is on the other end of the spectrum: pie-in-the-sky academicians who create companies that don't actually solve any real problems. The academicians stay in their one lane, publishing papers only at AI conferences and working with the same data sets for decades. But those data sets don't look like reality. They're stuck in the theoretical, doing all this academic work that can't solve the real problem.

I come from the world of science. I'm an academician. I've

published countless papers. I built a research lab of PhD students. I've done groundbreaking and record-breaking research, and my work has been inducted into the Hall of Fame of one of the top conferences in our area (pretenure). I say all this with humility, simply in an effort to show you that I know what it means to conduct "true" science.

But while Clinc has published top-tier papers in natural language processing and AI, that isn't our ultimate goal. We have a different way of looking at research and what is publishable. Most people publish based solely on intellectual merit. However, it actually behooves the research that you show both the intellectual merit *and* the metrics that provide evidence and validate those intellectual ideas.

This way of looking at research is ingrained in Clinc's DNA. It started with two professors, Lingjia, and me, all hell-bent on doing research and creating technologies that actually mattered for the future of society. Despite both of us being academicians, Lingjia and I have a surprisingly nonacademic culture between the two of us, by which I mean we aren't satisfied with publishing papers and going to conferences and talking among our elite academician peers to gain their respect. We prefer to focus on doing incredibly hard, interesting work that produces results that can be used by people in the world, work that can actually change something. That approach is why we are recognized by our peers as world-class scientists and researchers.

Our research is cross layered, meaning it crosses different aspects of technology. Other researchers don't typically do this. In academic culture, you usually stay in one lane and do that for your whole career. At Clinc, our core culture came from our academic lab, which is called Cross-Layer Architectures and Runtimes in Ten Years Lab, or CLARITY Lab. Our research perspective is centered on crossing different aspects of computer science, solving problems by threading things through each other, and covering multiple domains. We've built sophisticated systems that look at all aspects of AI technology, including the applications, models, and underlying platforms. It is systems research, AI research, and human-computer-interaction research. It is a host of different subareas of computer science that have to be solved together in order to solve the holy grail problem of AI.

FLIPPING THE MODEL

The labs at big companies also have top-notch researchers. And the companies themselves are entirely product focused. So why aren't their stellar researchers "productizing" their research the way we are?

The problem starts with the organizational model. The standard model is to have a research lab tacked on to the company. Microsoft Research is tacked on to Microsoft. Bell Labs is tacked on to Nokia. Thomas J Watson Research Center is tacked on to IBM. Intel Labs is tacked on to Intel. Facebook Research is tacked on to Facebook.

Traditionally, companies see these research labs as nice-to-haves, not must-haves. The labs are attached to existing companies that have already fully realized themselves. The labs are not integral to the company; they're ancillary, and they're dispensable. You can pluck out the research lab, and the company will still be a highly profitable engine that will continue to move things forward. You can even cut off the lab, and the company might actually end up stronger. Often, the labs are a financial burden to the business.

Why? Because these research labs are organized and structured to focus on fundamental research, meaning research that generates a paper. Sure, maybe they get a sponsor to try to bring that research into product. But most of the research stays fundamental and never actually gets made into a practical, usable product.

In the traditional model, research labs at these companies have to continuously work to justify their own existence and funding. The company generally views the lab as a money pit because it produces nothing useful for the company. Microsoft has mandated that its research lab will not cost more than 1 percent of the revenue of Microsoft.[3] If their revenues go down, they'll shrink the lab.

Google's DeepMind is a recent and perfect example. It's a massive lab, and Google is sinking millions of dollars into it. What have they created? Well, recently it was AlphaGo. AlphaGo is an AI that was able to beat the best human on the planet at the board game Go. Then, they created an AI that could play StarCraft, a strategic video game.

Inventions like this create marketing buzz. IBM's TJ Watson created an AI that could compete on *Jeopardy*. Years ago, they created Deep Blue, and it beat the greatest chess champion in the world. All these inventions were really cool. People loved them. They created great marketing campaigns and as such created value for their companies. But they're not creating any products that actually fuel the company's revenue. AlphaGo is cool, but DeepMind isn't producing anything of value for Google. So, for Google, it's a financial loss.

IBM's TJ Watson had a high focus on basic research. Bell Labs was all basic research. They published great papers and turned them into patents. There was Nobel Prize–winning work coming out of that lab. It was great that these researchers could just research and write papers all day, but no effective products were being made. So, eventually the labs were wound down.

Microsoft recently laid off their Silicon Valley lab, including

---

3   Larry Greenemeier, "How Microsoft's 1 Percenters Balance Basic Research with Short-Term Success," *Scientific American*, December 27, 2013, scientificamerican.com/article/microsoft-research-lee-qa/.

several Turing Award winners. The Turing Award is like the Nobel Prize for computer science, but Microsoft was okay laying off these incredible scientists because the research aspect was dispensable. It wasn't worth the high cost of paying these scientists what they're worth.

Bell Labs is regarded as one of the most sophisticated research labs in history. There are a number of Nobel Prize winners who worked in Bell Labs. But Bell Labs no longer exists. AT&T decided it was not an effective use of capital, because it wasn't creating value for the company.

In order to counter this, companies try to mandate productizing what their researchers are doing in the lab. "I don't care about your papers," the companies say. "I don't care about your contributions to the world. Get it into product and prove its value to the company."

That's what Microsoft tried to do. At one time, Microsoft Research was regarded as the top research lab for computer science. It was incredibly prestigious, the Stanford of research labs. The way it was structured, the lab was in a separate building from the rest of the company. In the lab, when you were working on your research, what you were really working toward was a paper. You had your idea, you did the research, and you wrote the paper. Great.

Then, you had a mandate: to productize that research. You had to go to the business side and find the businessperson who was already working on whatever you were working on. If your idea was about making the OS faster, you had to go to the operating system product team and find someone who wanted to implement your research into their product.

In this system, the onus was on the researcher to find a buyer, someone who would invest time and energy and money into prototypes and further research. But there wasn't any incentive for that product team to disrupt their work or distract themselves with your hoity-toity idea. They had their own mission: to get promoted or simply do their own thing. Implementing your idea was not on their agenda.

This also created a cultural divide; the scientists in the research lab were seen as living in la-la land, playing around with theoretical ideas that didn't have any basis in reality. Why would a product team want to waste time on something that might not even work when they had real product goals that were going to get them promoted?

It was an arduous task for a researcher to find some open-hearted person to divert resources to implement their research. It was a broken, ineffective system. But it was the way technology labs had worked forever, and it was an incredibly hard problem to solve from a business organizational standpoint. And often, when companies tried to solve it, their researchers ended up leaving.

That's what happened at Microsoft.

Google is trying to figure out right now how to reorganize DeepMind after the marketing boost they got from AlphaGo. But I'll bet you they're going to follow what Microsoft did and take that same organizational approach: "Go find a stakeholder and justify your existence to Google by finding somewhere to create value." You've got product people trying to integrate the work coming from the researchers, instead of the researchers doing work and trying to get it into product. It's product first versus technology first, and it usually fails.

This is why, when we started planning Clinc, we asked ourselves, "What would happen if we flip the model?"

What if we made the company a research lab and had the product be a vehicle for evaluating the validity of the research? What if the research is not dispensable, and we create an organizational structure around it where we're continuously flowing intellectual research ideas into product because product is a vehicle to evaluate the research? What if the product is a platform for testing whether the research makes sense? What if the metric we care about is creating value for the world? And what if we include that metric when measuring the merit of our ideas?

Instead of research being a tack on, organizationally and conceptually, research is at the core of the Clinc Lingjia and I created. Organizationally, the product is a layer for evaluating that research. The way we work, everything we do in our product is research, including the methodology of how to train AI.

We can publish that paper—the methodology of how to collect and curate data. But first, we test it in an actual usable product. Part of our evaluation metric is that it's working in the world, commercially, in people's lives. The criterion of evaluation for that research is product success. In our model, the research isn't done until we've evaluated it with the product. Our product is a rigorous platform for us to prove everything we're promising in the research.

Our product team is manifesting our research. We don't invent things and then productize it. We invent things in the build-out of our product. We invent things while solving problems for the real world, and then later we publish a paper about it.

To create these products, nobody had to find a stakeholder in order to productize their research. Everything we do in the research lab, every project we take on, once it's successful on its intellectual merit, is on the rails to go into product. It has to. Why? Because the problem we're trying to solve is so difficult, there is no product road map without research. The entire road map is driven by the research itself, because the problem is unsolved.

The problem mandates the research.

A MODEL BUILT FOR THE AI REVOLUTION

To my knowledge, when we created and implemented this model, it was the only organizational manifestation of its type. Our success with it stemmed from our insight that almost every problem in AI is a research problem. I think that is why Clinc dominated the top companies in the market working on conversational AI.

The AI revolution is a different beast than other recent technological revolutions. The internet was a revolution, but manifesting the value of the internet after its creation doesn't involve true technical invention. The internet is there. You can create a website, drive traffic to it, and put up ads. You can find standard talent to create the value of that revolution.

Smartphone apps were the next revolution, but again, you didn't need research to manifest value out of that revolution. It required standard software engineering. A new language for a new product, yes, but it's still programming. It's still dealing with the notion of buttons, of interfaces; they're simply for apps instead of websites.

Now, we're in the AI revolution. The reason we're not seeing the same rapid contagious success when it comes to manifesting value is because almost anything you want to do has to be invented. And so far, the inventions aren't working that well, particularly where conversational AI is concerned.

This is why the environment of this revolution is different from the prior two. In the internet revolution, it was sufficient to be a well-trained programmer. That allowed you to create interesting products and move the landscape forward, like Mark Zuckerberg did with Facebook and Jeff Bezos did with Amazon. Being a programmer was sufficient to solve those problems and create those technologies that could change the world.

The same was true with the mobile revolution. Steve Jobs and Apple invented the smartphone, which led to a whole generation of smartphones. To create technologies on that smartphone, you just need a well-trained programmer.

AI is completely different, because in order to innovate and create world-changing technologies, being a programmer isn't sufficient. Around 2005, there were a slew of articles about the massive shortage of folks who knew machine learning. Apple couldn't find people to hire. Google couldn't find people to hire. Throughout the world, there was a shortage of people who knew how to wield these technologies—and that continues today.

This is largely due to the fact that the pedagogy taught in undergrad for computer scientists is almost wholly devoid of the kind of AI technologies needed. It's widely known that Google spent $500 million in stock options recently to hire a professor in AI because there's such a shortage.

There's a shortage because we're at a time when innovating technology requires a higher level of expertise and knowledge of what's possible at the absolute frontier of science and research. That's the only way to move technology forward.

> We don't know how to build what we're building, and that necessitates innovation.

In this kind of environment, there's an opportunity to create a new structure. The way we've approached the creation of Clinc is a new kind of model for an era in which being a well-trained programmer is not sufficient to create the innovation and technology that moves society forward. You have to be an absolute scientist and invent the solutions.

The AI revolution mandates invention for every "productization" idea. People know how to build mobile apps. You just have to build one that does cool stuff and has cool features, and you're set. We don't know how to build what we're building, and that necessitates innovation. Every offering we make requires an invention from a PhD-grade trained computer scientist. We have to research and innovate and invent as we go, because it's never been done before.

GOALPOST: THE HUMAN IN THE ROOM

When we started Clinc, we started from scratch. We didn't start with the technology already in existence. We didn't even start with the technology Lingjia and I had already invented.

Instead, we started with a goalpost: the human in the room.

Most start-ups work under the mission of wanting to be better than the next guy. They look at their neighbors, at their competitors, at other companies and start-ups working on the same problems and say, "I want to do something better than those guys."

That is not the culture of Clinc. Clinc wasn't forged with that goal of competing in the market and bettering the competition. Instead, the company's DNA started with setting a goalpost—building an experience that's like talking to a human in the room—and trying to reach that post, a post that is a much greater leap than simply being better.

This meant we had no problem throwing all the status quo know-how in the trash and starting from fundamental research and science in order to build this thing authentically. We had to innovate and research how to take this deep-learning approach end to end, with all of its tenets, to create something that's viable, that can work for real. We have a completely new stack, built with new components, that has never been platformized before. It didn't exist until we invented it.

We would never have reached that point of invention if we were just trying to do what other start-ups were doing, only better. That's why we don't evaluate ourselves against the market. In fact, the first time we really looked at what our competitors were doing was when investors forced us to. They said, "Tell us how you're different."

"Well, damn," we said. "I guess we have to look into antiquity to describe how we're different." We never built ourselves to be different. We never built Clinc to be "better," to beat someone else. We built it to achieve our goal: the human in the room. So we don't evaluate ourselves based on how far ahead we are of the competition; that could lead to a false satisfaction of being a little better than the best crap out there. We evaluate ourselves based on how far we are from our goalpost, from the human in the room, from that level of understanding.

All these factors have come together to create Clinc's completely unique DNA. That DNA allows us to have expertise in creating a lab, creating a product, solving problems across domains, building large systems, and bringing in great talent. It's a DNA unlike that of any other company in the world—which makes Clinc a weird organism in an environment where you have thousands of these organisms competing for crabs in a bucket. Instead of squabbling with the rest, we're flying away, because we're aiming at that goalpost of human-in-the-room-level understanding, and we've got the minds and the organizational model to make it happen.

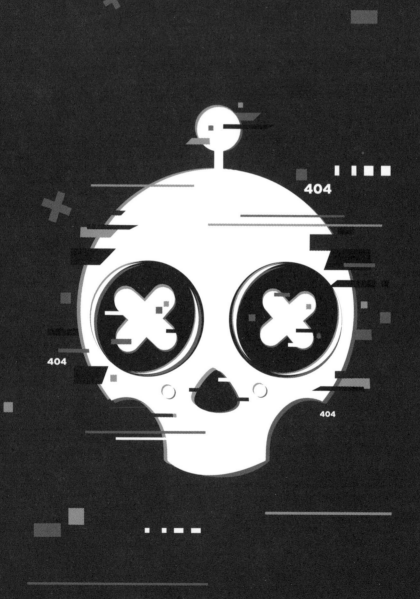

CHAPTER 5

THE BIRTH OF THE REVOLUTION

THE BOT HEARD ROUND THE WORLD

To understand why what we have built is different from anything else available on the market, let's take a step back and look at the larger AI landscape—going all the way back to the first AI bot heard around the world: Siri.

For decades before the first virtual assistant became available, the market was ready for innovation. People were ready for a conversational AI experience. But nothing became commercially viable in a significant way to create that shift in the way humans interact with technology—until Siri.

Various companies had been trying to create a commercially viable conversational AI, but none of them had been doing it all that well. One of those companies was the venerable research institute

SRI. In 2007, SRI created a spin-off company called Siri, Inc., born out of their CALO (Cognitive Assistant that Learns and Organizes) project, which according to SRI is the largest artificial intelligence effort in US history.[4]

I had a conversation with their original leadership and learned something interesting about Siri, Inc.: when the company started, they made near zero money. They couldn't get enterprises to pursue conversational AI seriously, so they weren't able to generate revenue. The company was in distress, with no choice but to sell. So, in 2010, SRI sold Siri, Inc. to Apple.

Using the technology developed by Siri, Inc., Apple created a product version of conversational AI in their mobile device, first as an app, and then included in the iPhone 4S released in 2011. Not only was Siri compelling enough for people to use it, its functions were sticky enough that people *kept* using it. They came to rely on it for specific tasks. As MG Siegler wrote for TechCrunch, "I think this is a feature that will sell the device. And I think all of Apple's rivals will have to act quickly to counter it. We've all seen the science fiction television shows and films where people talk to their computers like human beings and the computer understands them. That future is now."[5]

Siri was the catalyst that changed the whole trajectory of the way technology was developed. It created a ripple effect in the market, a voracious appetite for conversational AI. After Apple sparked the imagination of consumers with Siri, everybody started jumping in the

---

4 "Siri Launches Virtual Personal Assistant for IPhone 3GS," SRI International, February 5, 2010, https://www.sri.com/newsroom/press-releases/siri-launches-virtual-personal-assistant-iphone-3gs.

5 MG Siegler, "The IPhone 4S: Faster, More Capable, And You Can Talk To It," *TechCrunch* (blog), October 11, 2011, http://social.techcrunch.com/2011/10/11/iphone-4s-review/.

game. The demand was so immediately clear, interest was so immediately rampant, that the biggest companies in the world all got on board. Google, always in competition with Apple, introduced their offer, Google Now, in 2012. Then, in 2016 they introduced a new and improved version called Google Assistant. In 2015, Facebook got in with M, which functioned inside Facebook Messenger.

In 2014, in the midst of this flood of virtual assistants, Amazon changed the game by introducing Alexa and the Amazon Echo. It was a brilliant idea: a virtual personal assistant not just on your phone but right there in your home. You can walk into any room in your house, and there's your assistant, ready to help. Alexa is a great product idea, and it's been fueling and driving innovation and changing the landscape of consumer expectation. By 2016, Google had Google Home, their own in-home virtual assistant device featuring Google Assistant. In 2017, Apple announced its version, HomePod.

As the virtual assistant revolution took over the market, it didn't take long for businesses to catch on to the fact that people want to interact with technology in a conversational way. Enterprises across the world—from financial services to fast-food restaurants, from car companies designing in-car experiences to healthcare providers creating applications to aid doctors in their work—want to provide conversational experiences with their technology to their consumers.

A lot of companies tried to fill this desire with chatbots. When chatbots were first introduced, the intention was to use natural language. You would text the bot a sentence, and it would interact with you. But that quickly devolved into button pushing: the chatbot asks you questions and presents you with seven buttons you can push. Or it will say, "What do you want to ask? Pick A, B, or C." That's not really any different than point-and-click buttons. That's not conversational AI.

For true conversational AI, you need a platform. Here it's probably helpful to taxonomize the landscape a bit. You have virtual assistants, built-out product-based experiences that have names such as Alexa, Google Assist, Cortana, and Siri. These have a particular set of capabilities and knowledge.

Then, you have the platforms on which these virtual assistants are built: the technology stack with which you can create your own virtual assistant. There are many offerings available for building chatbots or virtual assistants—and they're all pretty far behind the curve. In fact, even companies that have their own virtual assistants, like Amazon and Google, don't use the same platforms for their products they offer to others.

For example, Google Assistant isn't built on Google's virtual assistant builder platform, Dialogflow. Dialogflow is an entirely separate product. It's a completely different technology stack, and that's what they offer for enterprises or individuals to build their own virtual assistants. To build Google Assistant, Google had a team of PhD-wielding scientists hand-building models to create that experience—and it's still not as good as what is possible with the best science.

When it comes to what they can actually build, enterprises are at a massive disadvantage. They don't have their own teams of data scientists, natural language processing experts, or machine-learning PhDs to hand-build their virtual assistants for them. They don't even have access to platforms like the one used to build Google Assist. They only have access to platforms like Dialogflow. As a result, they can't get the same level of quality in their consumers' eyes as, say, Google Assistant or Alexa—and, of course, even Siri, Google Assistant, and Alexa are not quite good enough in their consumers' eyes either.

NOT THERE YET

From their first appearance, people noticed the shortcomings of these virtual assistants. Reviews for Siri, along with praise, also had critiques. David Pogue gushed in the *New York Times* that Siri was "a crisply accurate, astonishingly understanding, uncomplaining, voice-commanded minion," but acknowledged, "She is not, however, as smart as *Star Trek*'s computers. She draws an apologetic blank" in response to certain questions and commands.[6] *Ars Technica* pointed out this issue as well, with Jacqui Cheng writing, "As Apple suggests, we began breaking away from our stiffer commands ('call Leah') to Siri and speaking to it (her?) as if she *were* a real person—only to be ripped out of the fantasy by something that Siri has so badly misinterpreted that it's easier to just think, 'I'll do it myself.'"[7]

By most reviewers' assessments, Google Assistant and Alexa surpass their predecessor, Siri, in their ability to understand what people say to them—but they are still not quite there. Reviewing the Echo for *The Verge*, David Pierce wrote, "She doesn't work every time, she doesn't respond the way she's supposed to half the time, and it doesn't take long before you stop totally relying on her. And then she sits silent."[8] He recounted similar flaws in his review of Google Home for *Wired*, writing, "Sometimes Home feels like sci-fi magic.

---

6   David Pogue, "IPhone 4S Conceals Sheer Magic," *The New York Times*, October 11, 2011, sec. Personal Tech, https://www.nytimes.com/2011/10/12/technology/personaltech/iphone-4s-conceals-sheer-magic-pogue.html.

7   Jacqui Cheng, "IPhone 4S: A Siri-Ously Slick, Speedy Smartphone," Ars Technica, October 18, 2011, https://arstechnica.com/apple/reviews/2011/10/iphone-4s-a-siri-ously-slick-speedy-smartphone.ars.

8   David Pierce, "Amazon Echo Review: Listen Up," The Verge, January 19, 2015, https://www.theverge.com/2015/1/19/7548059/amazon-echo-review-speaker.

Sometimes it reaches beyond its grasp and falls flat."[9]

Over at CNET, Dan Ackerman had a more favorable review of the Echo, but concluded by saying, "When something just sort of works as you expect it to, without needing a lot of specialized tinkering or workarounds, that's what counts as a breakthrough product these days."[10] That's a far cry from expecting excellence from our conversational AI. As Pierce wrote in his Google Home review, "You'll like them both, though neither is perfect. The question is how much you're willing to bet on what these devices could be, and which company you think can deliver on that promise."[11]

The fact is, all these products and platforms are a long way from delivering on the full promise of conversational AI. Everyone knows, both intuitively and quantitatively, that we're not there yet. Everyone knows that these experiences are not yet all they can be. When we interact with them, we don't really trust them to work. They're often brittle. They can do only the simplest of things. They're acceptable enough that we want to use them, but talking to these devices doesn't feel like talking to a human. These companies are simply in a rat race, trying to be better than their competitors.

We want to interact with a resilient interface that can understand us even if we're messy, even if we say things in not quite the right way or in unexpected ways, or even if we make a mistake and go back to correct ourselves. In other words, we want them to be able to understand us when we speak like human beings. As they

---

9   David Pierce, "Google Home Review: A Smart Speaker That's Pretty Great—And Crazy Ambitious," *Wired*, November 3, 2016, https://www.wired.com/2016/11/review-google-home/.

10   Dan Ackerman, "Why I Think Amazon's Echo Is the Breakthrough Product of 2015," CNET, December 20, 2015, https://www.cnet.com/news/amazon-echo-and-alexa-the-most-impressive-new-technology-of-2015/.

11   Pierce, "Google Home Review."

stand now, those virtual assistants can understand only rigid, robotic, one-shot commands: "Order me an Uber." "Turn the lights on." "Set a timer." You can't have rich conversations navigating complex issues. You can't be a free-flowing human being.

To soften the blow, these devices include lots of cute Easter eggs. If you say, "Alexa, open the pod-bay doors," Alexa will respond, "I'm sorry, Dave; I can't do that." Siri will recite dad jokes and bad pickup lines. If you ask Google Home for "Tea. Earl Gray. Hot," it'll say, "The usual. Coming right up, Captain." They're fun; they're delightful; they go viral. But when it comes to their actual utility in peoples' lives, it's unclear how much—or how little—they can do.

When these products were presented to the public, they were touted as your virtual assistant. What wasn't really specified was the scope of what they can and can't do. Companies market the little ways it can solve problems in your life. Need the weather? Ask it the weather. Need to play a song? It can play you a whole radio station of that artist. Need to call your mother? You can say, "Call Mom," and it'll dial her up for you.

And as people have learned the phrases, questions, and commands needed to communicate with the various virtual assistants, they've became more integrated into people's daily patterns. But this still requires learning what commands and phrases the assistants can understand and what they can't. The purpose of technology is to decrease complexity, to make things simpler. If you have to memorize a whole list of precisely worded questions to ask, that's not really making things simpler, is it?

READY FOR MORE

In the years since Siri was first released, peoples' dissatisfaction has been growing. In each new generation of these virtual assistants, the same issues persist. We want something that can tolerate messiness, that can tolerate complexity, that can tolerate the free-form way humans communicate, that can tolerate taking the conversation wherever we want it to go. And it's incredibly frustrating when these conversational devices can't do that.

Think about the last time you spoke to someone who wasn't quite understanding you and kept asking, "What?" Think about that awkward, frustrating feeling of having to repeat yourself. You probably gave up eventually, right? If that happened every time you talked to that person, you would probably think, "I don't want to talk to that person again. It's such a painful experience."

> Being able to speak freely, as you would to a human in the room, is the holy grail of conversational AI.

It's part of the human psyche; we don't like to fail at interaction. We want to have robust and smooth interactions, not awkward and painful ones. It makes sense that we want the same thing with our technology. Being able to speak freely, as you would to a human in the room, is the holy grail of conversational AI. When we hit that, when humans can trust the experience and trust that the AI will understand them, it will be transformational.

And that's exactly what underlies the technical vision of Clinc. Despite the shortcomings of the products available to consumers, peoples' appetite for conversational AI is not waning. In fact, people want it more than ever. The usage rates of decent experiences—the

Alexas, the Google Homes, the Siris of the world—are actually ramping up.

One thing is clear: conversational AI is here to stay in a major way. Other hot technology trends have come and gone. A few years ago, everyone thought 3D television was going to be the next big thing. Every TV maker had their 3D TV offering. And sure, they sold some, but pretty soon people lost interest. Essentially, the experiment failed. Conversational AI products, on the other hand, are actually increasing in popularity year after year. In fact, the number of virtual assistants is forecast to exceed the current world population by 2021.[12] That's right—we're talking more AI than human beings within the next few years.

THE NEXT STEP

Where we are now with AI is similar to the early days of the internet. What we have with the AI currently available on the market is comparable to the first modem. That's the level of the experience. What we're working on at Clinc is providing the T1 line—the dedicated, advanced telephone line between service provider and client—that changes the game, and we're looking ahead all the way through to 5G.

To continue this internet analogy, let's use bandwidth as a stand-in for conversational complexity, depth, robustness, and resilience. When you have low bandwidth and try to stream a video, it comes out blurry and jerky. That's where conversational AI is now. We're creating the AI that will give you the smooth, 4K streaming equivalent of the AI experience.

---

12 Ronan De Renesse, "Virtual Digital Assistants to Overtake World Population by 2021," Ovum, May 17, 2017, https://ovum.informa.com/resources/product-content/virtual-digital-assistants-to-overtake-world-population-by-2021.

The next step after being able to ask complex, messily worded questions is having actual discussions, conversations with twists and turns and returns. To do this, you need to access not just the intelligence of understanding, but the intelligence of reasoning. So, machines will have to evolve into a class of intelligence that's characterized by reasoning.

The reasoning component is the frontier we're at now, the big challenge in getting us to that human level of understanding. Reasoning means the ability to navigate the logical complexities of interacting across multiple topics. It means being able to follow and forward the conversation no matter where it goes. In order to do this, machines will have to learn to understand partial information. That's a kind of intelligence almost like intuition.

Human intelligence leverages lived experience and intuition to understand things with which we're not familiar. If I start talking about a subject with which you're not familiar, you'll find a framework in which to understand it. We usually do this by analogies. If a physicist says to you, "Imagine the speed of light," you might have trouble wrapping your mind around that concept. But if they say, "Imagine you could run as fast as a beam of light," you can build a framework. You might not know what a photon is, but you know what it means to run alongside something, and that analogy will help you build a framework on which you can build an understanding. You can then apply that understanding to the beam of light.

This is a much harder problem to solve. It requires leaving behind the old way of doing things and embracing a new and better science: machine learning.

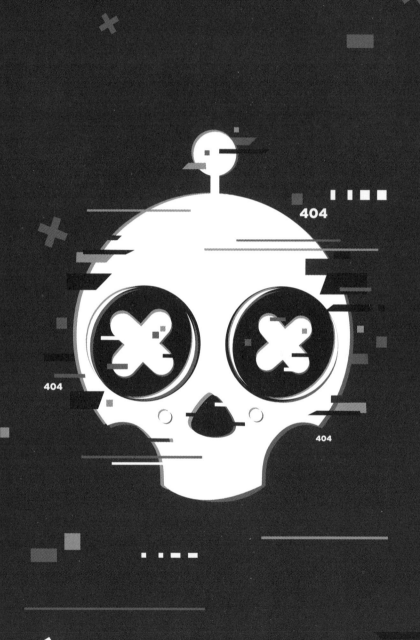

CHAPTER 6

THE NEURAL NETWORK UPRISING

NEURAL NETWORKS: THE POWER OF THE BRAIN

Conversational AI is hot for everybody. The top four companies on the planet—Google, Apple, Amazon, and Microsoft—are all investing substantial resources into solving the holy grail problem of conversational AI. Thousands of other companies in the world are also trying to crack it. It's what the market is demanding.

And yet, when you look at the quality of the AI experience and the sophistication of the technology, there hasn't been much change or improvement in what's available on the market. Even though there is significant investment from all these companies, the technology is not advancing in a way we can really feel. Why is that?

To understand where the technology is currently and where it needs to go, let's zoom out and start with the big picture: What is artificial intelligence?

AI encompasses any kind of approach to having machines or computers simulate human intelligence. One class of approaches uses machine learning; these approaches for AI applications are based on models that learn from data. In machine learning, data sets are used to train models to capture intelligence in some way, shape, or form.

Machine learning is a theoretical subfield of computer science. Computer science has many subfields. You've got operating systems, compilers, and programming languages, to name a few. These are all practical, applicable fields. You've also got subfields that are theoretical. Machine learning is fundamentally one of those theoretical subfields. It's a subfield that can be explored in the absence of applications. The work can happen theoretically and mathematically, not necessarily in practical application.

Then you have subfields that are application focused, like computer vision—how machines see. Another subfield that is fundamentally an application inside the sphere of AI is natural language processing: computers understanding and generating human language. These application subfields utilize various AI approaches, including machine learning. Machine learning has come to dominate computer vision, and it is now beginning to permeate and dominate natural language processing as well.

There are a host of approaches for natural language processing. Approaches in one set are rules based on and inspired by computational linguistics, in which a sequence of steps using formal representation of language structure simulate intelligence. Another subset of approaches uses deep learning, or deep neural networks. Deep neural network approaches (a subset of machine learning) are the set of techniques that simulate the way neurons work in the brain.

In the brain, neurons are all interconnected. A sequence of neurons firing leads to the classification of that data. Deep-learning or deep neural network approaches are geared toward capturing information in the way our human brains capture information. In a deep neural network approach, we simulate synapses and activation functions. The function of a neuron communicating information is simulated in a mathematical model in the computer.

Here's a simplified illustration of the difference between a rules-based approach and a deep-learning approach, in the field of computer vision. A rules-based approach would be training a computer to recognize images of Superman by an *S* on the chest, a red cape, and red boots. The model would learn those rules in a supervised way, being given a coded list of attributes to recognize Superman. The problem is, there are so many ways those rules could go wrong. Perhaps in the image Superman is standing in such a way that you can't see the full *S* on his chest. Perhaps the image is in black and white, and you can't tell that the boots and cape are red.

A neural networking approach, by contrast, would be to give the AI hundreds of pictures of Superman and let the neural network learn on its own, without predefined features. This is deep learning: using data to extract the unknown, to capture learning in a way you can't point to. I can't point to the five neurons in your head that are the "identifying Superman" neurons. That's not how it works. It's actually the interconnectedness in capturing the emergent properties of Superman that allows your brain to identify him.

This is what neural networking captures, and it's what makes deep learning so powerful. But if it's so powerful, why is it only just starting to be commercially utilized today?

THE DEEP-LEARNING REVOLUTION

Machine-learning techniques, like deep learning and neural networks, were discovered in rudimentary forms decades ago, but for the longest time they've been relegated to academic investigation. They haven't led to any actual technology or real commercial realization.

Then, around 2010, there was a surge in machine-learning approaches becoming commercially relevant that has continued through today. The confluence of many evolutions in technology has led to an environment that can sustain commercially interesting applications of deep learning, which has in turn led to a tectonic plate shift in the world of AI technology.

The big reason for this shift is, fundamentally, the mobile internet revolution. Thanks to the mobile revolution and the social media revolution, we now have copious amounts of data from which AI can learn. The thing about neural network and deep-learning approaches is that you need a ton of data. Older approaches can learn more quickly with less data, but the amount of learning plateaus long before a deep-learning approach. Deep learning can easily surpass older approaches, but it needs a lot more data.

We carry around in our pockets the equivalent of a supercomputer of three decades ago.

Today, with there being cameras and microphones practically every-where, data is constantly being collected, and it often ends up in a cloud somewhere.

In addition to lots of data, deep-learning approaches require the computational power to train these models. The more data, the more computational power is needed. So, the other factor that makes deep learning applicable to real commercial use is the amount of computational power in the world today. We carry around in our pockets the equivalent of a supercomputer of three decades ago—and there are millions of them around the world.

Computer vision is the field in which deep learning has taken hold in the most powerful way. There was a time when computer vision was dominated by other approaches that didn't necessarily include neural networks. Then there was a revolution, largely pioneered by Google. I can't understate the impact they've had on the landscape and frontier of technology. Google's Cloud Vision API application is where deep learning started to take off when it comes to the commercial realization of what's possible.

Cloud Vision API is an open-source application programming interface (API) for image classification. Image classification is when an AI looks at an image and classifies it. It looks at a dog and says, "That's a dog." It looks at a chair and says, "That's a chair."

This ability to label images was done through a supervised learning approach using ImageNet—a massive, crowdsourced visual database. The database contains millions of images that have been hand annotated, meaning the images are labeled and classified by human beings. That database is used to train programs like Cloud Vision to recognize images.

ImageNet and Cloud Vision were incredibly impactful in popularizing computer vision as a field dominated by deep-learning approaches. This kind of image recognition was then applied to facial recognition, with Facebook doing some seminal work in that area. Now, the commercial way people do facial recognition is with deep learning.

These projects have started to move deep learning from the academic sphere to the commercial sphere. It's the same thing that happened with autonomous driving systems. That work started in the academic sector, at MIT, but it has now become huge in the commercial milieu. This is essentially what Google did with its commercial ambition to bring what was strictly research to life.

The AI economy we're in today has been fueled by the discovery that deep learning can take us leaps and bounds further than older approaches, thanks to the confluence of all of these factors: the availability of data, the computational power of modern technology, and the commercial ambitions of companies like Google and Facebook.

Unfortunately, while leaps forward have been made in the area of computer vision, the language-understanding sphere has trailed. In fact, it's about a decade behind the transformation happening in computer vision.

Why? To start, comparatively speaking, images are easy. Natural language, on the other hand, is a more complicated problem, because it's not as modular a problem. To create a conversational AI, there are numerous disparate problems that must be solved together in order to create one intelligent system.

In computer vision, there's one system for the problem of classification. In these cases, there is a single neural network that will tell you whether the image is a cat or a dog, Superman or Batman. It's one thing, and one model will tell you the outcome. Face recognition is similar; there is one neural network to tell you what face is in an image.

In order to understand human language, there are many problems that need to be solved in disparate ways. It's not as clean. There are problems automatically detecting paraphrases. There are problems with similarity analysis. There are problems with slot value extraction and pairing. With intent classification. With sentiment analysis. With information extraction.

There's the challenge of dialogue: following the twists and turns of a conversation, keeping context, remembering what was said before. If I say, "Are there any good restaurants in the area? Okay, which ones are Japanese? I also want a low price," the AI needs to be able to follow each of those and keep it in context.

There are a whole host of problems that you have to solve together in order to extract meaning out of what is said. How do you build an end-to-end system for many disparate problems that captures the human way of learning language? How you solve them together in a composite way impacts the resulting AI you create.

OVERTHROWING THE PEDAGOGY

There's no pedagogical or scientifically established way to solve these problems. There is no established best technique. You have to borrow ideas from different fields, spanning all the available tools, including both deep learning and other approaches. You have to construct the right system, the right composite approach, to solve all these problems together.

So, how do you do that? Well, that's a point of some contention. For a while now, there has been a fierce battle going on in natural language processing. For around fifty years, experts in the natural language processing field were doing things a certain way, a way that was heavily influenced by computational linguistics. Their approach was driven by applying the art of linguistics in a computational way. They had a host of linguistic approaches, none of which included deep learning.

The linguistic approach focuses on reasoning: the reason of grammar, the reason of synonyms, and so forth. You have to identify the nouns, verbs, and adjectives and create a formal framework for the reasoning behind language. Some popular linguistic approaches being used commercially utilize WordNet, which is a lexical database for the English language. Approaches that use WordNet are aligned with the top-down notion of understanding the relationships between words, coding synonyms and antonyms, and so forth.

These approaches are not consistent with the core understanding of deep learning, and they are not consistent with how humans learn or understand language. Humans are neural networks. We are deep learning. We learn from data. We learn from experiences. We listen to Mom and Dad and babysitters and teachers saying a lot of stuff, and we learn from that data. We learn English before we know what a verb is. When you're four years old, you don't know what a verb is. You don't know how to map synonyms. But you can understand complex, messy English sentences.

Even as adults, after we've studied English in school and learned all about parts of speech and sentence construction, we don't process language by saying, "First identify the nouns, verbs, and adjectives in the sentence. Understand what the noun phrase is, what the verb phrase is, and so on." Our brains don't actually pick out all the nouns, verbs, and adjectives. Instead, as we listen to someone speak, the words wash over our neural network, and we understand the full meaning of what is being said.

> **Instead of learning from rules, deep learning approaches learning from data.**

This is what deep learning and neural networking mimics. Instead of learning from rules, deep learning approaches learning from data. It's a completely different paradigm. If AI is meant to simulate human intelligence, it makes sense for AI to learn, process, and understand the way humans learn, process, and understand. So why is there a battle?

I contend politics is a factor. If you're a sixty-year-old professor who has been pioneering techniques in one paradigm for thirty years, when the paradigm shifts, your life's work becomes irrelevant. Nobody wants that. So, when the paradigm starts shifting, the people who have been working in the old paradigm tend to roll their eyes and say, "Oh, these crazy kids coming in with their crazy ideas." Even as I write this book, there are certain professors at my institution and others still rolling their eyes and saying, "Machine learning, deep learning, it's craziness. Computational Linguistics for Life! It's dogma!"

But what is beautiful about science is that at the end of the day, results are all that matter. The humanities and social sciences don't have this benefit. Politics do impact the ideations that happen. Biases and cultural norms and what's cool at the moment affect those fields. But in science, whatever works better is going to win. If something is working better than another thing, it's going to come out on top, no matter what you think.

Machine learning has demonstrated its ability to advance natural language processing. It's in my academic research and in the research of others. It's been presented at conferences. It's been written up in publications and papers. The evidence shows that it's working.

However, the current pedagogy still teaches people to take the computational linguistic approach. If you become a PhD in natural language processing today, you will come out trained with that pedagogy, with certain established norms as to how to approach this stuff. Certain principles are ingrained, giving you this mentality of using computational linguistics to solve these problems. The mentality can muddy your ability to build something better.

This is one reason people have had so much difficulty building this stuff; they are trained into a certain mindset. You have to unload that mindset and start with a fresh perspective. You have to start from scratch.

STARTING FROM SCRATCH

That's what we did at Clinc. We started from scratch, from the most fundamental pieces. Our stack avoids computational linguistics. It does not rely on nouns, verbs, and adjectives. It never knows what a synonym is. There's no coded way of saying, "These are the synonyms of this word." We never have rules.

There are many problems that need to be solved in tandem to create one AI. You can put deep learning in certain places and not in other places. There are different approaches to solve different problems. What approach we use for each problem comes organically.

Here are two examples of approaches we use to solve the challenge of understanding messy human language: slot extraction and embedding.

We use a recurrent neural network, or RNN, and transfer learning approach to slot value extraction that allows us to extract up to fourteen arbitrary slots from one messy utterance. The RNN is trained just with label data sets, much like the image classification problem, but instead of training the ability to recognize images of dogs, cats, or mice, we're training the ability to recognize arbitrary entities or slots.

What does that mean? Say we've got an AI trained in dinosaurs, and a new dinosaur has been discovered. I want the AI to be able to automatically and intuitively recognize new dinosaur names when they are invented. Imagine I said to you, a human, "I was running away from this yellow Macbookosaurus, and I didn't know what to do. I had to hide under a tree." Even though you've never heard the word before, you would be able to identify from the context that "Macbookosaurus" is a dinosaur. That is a slot value extraction. Even in those messy sentences, you can pick out the dinosaur.

A second slot value extraction would be identifying the color in the sentence. The old-school way for an AI to do that would be to train the AI on all of the colors, such as red, black, yellow, blue, and green. Then the AI would look for those words in the sentence.

But imagine if I said something like, "I thought the blackitude Macbookosaurus was chasing me, but it was just a red herring." The AI trained on the color words wouldn't be able to tell me what color the dinosaur was, because it would zero in on *red* and not on *blackitude*, a color I invented.

If I said that sentence to you, a human, you would immediately be able to tell that the dinosaur was *blackitude*, not because you know that *blackitude* is a color word or because you identified *blackitude* as an adjective, but because of the context. That's slot value extraction. *Blackitude* is not a real color, but you know from the sentence that it's likely a color. Your brain does that instantly.

What we do here is train that capability for slot value extraction or slot value pairing using RNN-based transfer learning. You can train it for anything—for dinosaurs, for cats, for cars.

Our stack can do fourteen such things in one messy utterance. You can give it a paragraph, and it will be able to say, "This is the dinosaur. That's the color of the dinosaur. That's the day the dinosaur chased you." In this way, we can extract fourteen slots from a single messy utterance without knowing sentence structure, nouns, verbs, adjectives, and so on.

We've also created a specialized unsupervised embeddings approach that enables the AI to understand words and phrases it's never heard before. These embeddings underly our transfer learning approaches. Typically, in order to do this, systems employ the notion of synonyms. The word *cup* has the synonyms *mug*, *glass*, and so on. In order for the AI to understand, you have to enumerate all the synonyms of *cup*. We leverage an approach in which you don't have to enumerate synonyms. Instead, the approach uses a technology, not used in those other systems, that allows automatic mapping. This means the AI can map the word *dinner* to restaurants, even if it doesn't know the word *dinner*.

For example, you may say, "I've got to take this friend out to dinner, and I think I'm gonna end up spending, like, five hundred dollars. Can I afford that?" In your budgeting, you probably don't have a Dinner category. But you probably do have a Restaurants or a Dining Out category. If you were talking to a human banker and you said, "I need to know what I spent on dinner last week," they would know to look at restaurant spending.

We want our AI to do the same thing. One approach to make that happen would be to list all the things that map to restaurants: *dinner*, *food*, *dine*, *eat*, and so on, creating a long, coded list. The embeddings approach doesn't require coming up with that coded list. Instead, without setting those rules, embedding lets the AI know that out of the spending categories of Restaurants, Electronics, and Makeup, the word *dinner* is most likely to map to Restaurants. If you said, "Cheeseburgers," embedding would allow the AI to know that Restaurants is the most likely category. If you said, "Mascara," it would map that to Makeup. If you said, "Phone," it would map to Electronics.

There are many ways to do embeddings. This particular model is trained by just letting it "read." You give it all of Wikipedia. You give it all of the *New York Times*. You give it all of the *Wall Street Journal*. You give it all the web pages of the internet. And you let it read the language and learn, in an unsupervised manner. The neural network learns from all that reading—just like in computer vision the neural network learns how to recognize Superman by looking at hundreds of images of Superman.

When the model reads all this language, it's able to build a framework from which it can understand things by placing them into an analogous relationship with things it already knows. It intuitively comes to understand that *dinner* goes with *restaurants*. It learns how close together words are and how they can be used. *Cat* and *dog*, for example, are closer together than *cat* and *refrigerator*. You could say, "My cat jumped over the rock" or "My dog jumped over the rock," and both would make sense. "My refrigerator jumped over the rock," not so much. *Cat* is more replaceable by *dog* than it is by *refrigerator*.

Embeddings are represented as a vector, as a point in multidimensional space. To understand it, let's imagine it in one-dimensional space. In one-dimensional space, things would have a numerical value. *Cat* might be 5, *dog* might be 6—very close to each other. *Refrigerator* would be further away—say, 52. In multiple dimensions, points in the space may be closer or farther away from other points. Clusters of points can also emerge.

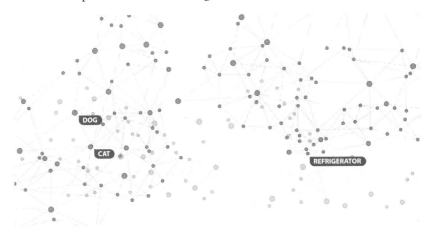

Restaurant, cheeseburger, dinner—all these words would be clustered close together. *Phone* would be farther away, closer to the cluster that includes *electronics, charger, computer*, and so on. *Mascara* would be far from both of those clusters, closer to the cluster with *makeup, blush, lipstick*, and so on. When you say something close to one of those clusters, the model will be able to make a prediction of where to categorize that thing.

WORDS, WORDS, WORDS

The AI learns this model by reading those billions of words. It's a neural network trained by reading, and it's a very powerful approach. You can leverage embeddings to allow those mappings for the entire language, no matter what is said. You train a neural network to listen to stuff and know what it is.

We've also pioneered—and patented—a methodology to train our AI based on a powerful tool: crowdsourcing.

For the approaches commonly used by the existing commercially available technologies that do conversational AI, you have to manually enter different ways you can ask a question in order to train the AI—for instance, four or five different ways of asking to turn on the lights. But that only creates a very brittle experience, because the AI will be trying to match keywords to those four or five specific ways of asking the question. It's following those specific rules. If you don't ask in one of those five ways, it won't be able to understand you.

Our AI doesn't learn from rules. Like a kid, it learns from a data set. That means you have to collect robust data sets from which it can really learn how humans talk. Doing that manually is impossible. If I ask you to come up with ten different ways you can ask about how much money you spent last week, I guarantee you will only be able to come up with maybe four or five different ways. You'll run out of ideas way before ten.

But you're just one person. If we ask a hundred people, we'll come up with far more than ten ways of asking. If we ask a thousand, we'll come up with even more. The larger the data set, the more different permutations of the question you'll have, and the more the AI can learn, to the point where you could ask the question literally any way you want and it would understand you.

To get AI to learn at that level, you have to give it hundreds and sometimes thousands of examples of how people actually talk in the real world. How do you give it a data set that big and robust? And how do you build that into a platform that really works?

In order to do this, we had to integrate a particular set of methodologies no other platform has around crowdsourcing. Crowdsourcing is a method of gathering data in which you send out the small task—like ways to ask a question—to ten thousand people and pay them pennies to complete the task and send it back to you. Google leveraged this kind of crowdsourcing for their image-classification work. They sent images to thousands of people and paid them a few cents for every photo they tagged with "cat," "dog," or whatever image was in the photo. Thanks to crowdsourcing, Google now has millions of pictures labeled without having to put in a huge amount labor themselves, which would have been an impossible task.

We've developed a methodology that seamlessly integrates crowdsourcing into our platform and automates data collection and generation using this powerful tool. When you're building your AI on our platform, you can get tens of thousands of people to give you diverse examples. The methodologies we've designed around this innovation do not exist on any other platform.

Now, when you get these massive crowdsourced data sets, you're inevitably going to end up with some bad examples that could diminish the intelligence of your AI. It's like teaching a kid with a bad example. You don't want to teach your kid that the way to wash your hands after using the restroom is to lick them. But how are you supposed to weed out the bad examples from the thousands of examples you've crowdsourced? That would be incredibly laborious to do by hand.

So, we researched and invented a way to automatically read through all the data and pull out the weird examples. We worked on it for three months, and then we wrote a paper on it and had it published in a top journal. We patented it, and now it's a product in our platform: an AI that will read your data and pull out the weird ones. So, if you've collected ten thousand utterances automatically with crowdsourcing, you can push a button and automatically see all the bad examples, and then get rid of them. This is a strong example of the value of the research to product organization of the company.

We invented this, published it, and now it's in the product creating value for our customers. We have more than a dozen examples like this, all patented. In the four years since we launched the company, we have continued to invent things, meaning we are continuing to increase the technology gap between our platform and the rest of the market. We call it the technology moat.

I haven't seen competing products innovating over time. They're still using antiquated computational linguistics-based techniques. As I continuously survey the market looking for what might be coming up next, all I see is the moat increasing.

BUILDING BLOCKS

You can utilize approaches like we use for slot extraction and embeddings for many things. Indeed, these building blocks can be misused to train a model to identify nouns, verbs, and adjectives in a sentence. In fact, there has been work on using deep learning to train models to identify nouns, verbs, and adjectives, and you could say this AI uses deep learning. However, I contend that in this case the core principles of biologically inspired deep learning are being abused to support the paradigm on using those same linguistic rules. It's still resorting to grammar, and you're right back into a model for understanding language that isn't truly capturing the way humans understand language.

Embedding and slot value extraction are just the first steps in building this kind of intelligence in AI. At Clinc, we have had an incredibly rich approach to what's called dialogue management—how you allow context and what has been learned so far to determine where to take the conversation next. Our approach is based on both context graphs and the coupling of dialogue management and response logic. After all, responses can be structured based on context as well as information. You can have completely divergent responses based on the context you've built so far, the semantics you've learned through the turns of the conversation. The conversation can go in entirely different directions. So you have to separate the logic of a conversation from the response that comes next, allowing conversations to go in any direction. This requires a special kind of graph in which you encode logic or dialogue management, and then another system to determine how you respond based on the context collected so far.

There are two additional massive problem domains for conversational AI: the ability to reason, which enables interesting interactions; and the ability to use intuition and experience. Understanding how to use a generalized notion of context to figure out what to say next or where the dialogue is going is one small piece toward a fully complex reasoning capability. It's part of the bigger next step: using experience and intuition to steer the intelligence in the conversation and allowing for the reasoning that happens in a sophisticated conversation. Those pieces must be on the horizon for human-in-the-room interactions, and deep learning brings great promise in solving these problems.

The approach to all these problems represents tools and components to construct AI. Deep learning is the nuts and bolts and wood. What you can build with it all depends on how you utilize those materials. You can build structures that are unstable, that can break, that quickly reach their limit. Or you can build structures that are strong and powerful, that push technology forward, that can create AI far beyond what's widely commercially available today—structures that give people the AI experience they truly desire.

CHAPTER 7

TO THE ENDS OF THE EARTH

Groundbreaking technology and unique DNA have made Clinc what it is, but there's another factor as well: our relationships with the institutions we work with. One thing that is always true of Clinc is that we go to the ends of the earth to deliver, no matter how complex the institution. We're able to do that because we care about building relationships. We care about the mission, not just your money. We want to change the world with you. We want you to get four promotions at your company for bringing us in. We want to see our technology in the hands of your customers, making their experience with your company even better. Our interests are aligned.

I'll tell you the story of one of our relationships to give you an idea of what I mean. It's a banking institution I'll call "Pubclays."

A SCRAPPY START

Our first bank customer was US-AY-AY, while one of our largest is Pubclays. Like our experience with US-AY-AY, securing Pubclays as a client wasn't easy.

Pubclays, like US-AY-AY, wanted conversational AI. They wanted to automate their processes, save money by taking calls out of the call center, and be relevant. The relevancy was triggered by a trend: most financial institutions were trying to implement some kind of virtual assistant.

Across the market, there were (and still are) many different approaches being tried to get this kind of work done. During the mobile revolution, when all the banking institutions were creating their mobile apps for smartphones, the phase one approach was to hire vendors to build the apps for them. Then they would launch the app to market.

Then, as smartphones and apps became more sophisticated, banks found it too expensive to make customizations to their apps. They wanted to control what their customers experienced, and every time they wanted to make a change, they'd have to bring the vendor in at a steep cost. So the biggest banks created app teams in-house. They hired people who were mobile-app developers and brought that capability within the company.

This was the exact same journey the banks went through with websites. First, they hired third parties to build them, then they brought those teams in-house. And today, that remains the status quo. The largest banks, and even some medium-size banks, have teams in-house that build out all their mobile apps and websites. So, interestingly, banks are, in a way, slowly evolving to become technology companies.

Today, as conversational AI comes into demand, the institutions feel like it makes sense to take the same approach. Many banks have tried to build a team internally, but based on all the challenges we've been talking about, none of them have been very successful. All new products require innovation, and conversational AI in particular requires the world's best minds: PhDs and scientists. Conversational AI isn't just another kind of technological product they can build in-house.

Developing a team in-house is one approach, but the challenges in that approach are why banks have started turning back to their previous model: working with vendors. Banks already work with vendors in other technological areas. For example, many banks will use vendors for personal financial management tools (PFMs), which show the analytics of your transactions. Most banks don't build those in-house. And when it comes to AI, banks are now starting to leave behind the in-house model as well.

Pubclays was deep into a vendor journey when they encountered Clinc. They had been working with IPsoft's Amelia product for about six months, and they'd had nothing but pain and frustration. So they had decided to look at the market and conduct a rigorous RFP (request for proposals) to find the right vendor.

Initially, Pubclays sent RFPs to around thirty-nine companies— of which Clinc was not one. That is, until someone reached out to us through our website.

"Hey, we want to learn a little more about you," the message said. The person behind that message happened to see an article about us in *Forbes* that was published in October of 2016 and figured it wouldn't hurt to have us throw our hat into the ring.

Now, usually when an institution puts out an RFP, somebody there already has their favorite choice. My hypothesis is that IPsoft was Pubclays's favorite. And when that is the case, the RFP normally is written with that vendor in mind. But the institution needs to do their due diligence so they can check the box saying they did so, and that was fine with us. No matter what the reason the door had been opened, it was open, and we needed to take advantage of the opportunity.

From forty vendors, Pubclays cut the RFP down to twenty-eight, and we received an email saying, "We've selected you for the next round of our RFP." They asked us to do a few more things, then they cut the list some more, as it was a tournament. We eventually made it to the final eight, which is when Pubclays asked us to prove ourselves by building a prototype of what we could offer.

Building a prototype requires a lot of work from our engineers, and we had a very staunch policy that we don't do anything for free. After all, people don't value what they don't have to pay for. People need to put some skin in the game in order to really show commitment.

So, we told Pubclays, "Hear you; no." We were not going to build them something for free.

"But we aren't paying any of the other potential vendors," Pubclays told us. It turns out, many folks in the market don't have our rule. They'll do free work for companies just to earn their business. But we knew that we had the real thing, the actual goose that lays the golden eggs.

Pubclays countered by saying they didn't have the business processes to be able to pay us for the RFP. After a number of tough conversations, we told them we'd have to withdraw from consideration.

And they relented.

We were the only vendor they paid, and they did it by having lower-level employees at the bank each put $10,000 on their corporate credit cards, which the company then expensed. Why did they do it? Because they'd already seen a glimpse of what Clinc could do, and they wanted us to get to the next phase.

We built our prototype, and we proved that we could build what we promised. After that phase, Pubclays was down to the final four vendors: us, Nuance's Nina, a local shop in Britain, and IPsoft's Amelia, the one they already had, which probably had someone internally championing them.

Clinc was by far the smallest of the four companies. Nuance and IPsoft each probably have ten thousand employees. They're public companies. I don't know much about the British company, but they were certainly bigger than we were. At the time, we had only about fifteen people in the company. It was completely crazy, but Pubclays knew how small we were.

For the final four evaluations, Pubclays wanted all the companies to come on-site in the UK and give one-hour presentations centered on what we had built for them. Here's a little-known secret: whenever I do presentations, I'm always nervous. I look so comfortable on stage or in customer meetings, but I'm usually pretty terrified. My cortisol is way up; my heart is racing; I'm stressed out for probably four hours before anything happens. I'm like a boxer before a match, punching myself in the face to try to psyche myself up. Then, as soon as I'm on stage, after the first five minutes, I'm like, "All right, cool. This is fine. I've got this." I find my groove.

So, before this final presentation for Pubclays, I was nervous as hell, and I had reason to be. First, we had an Amazon Echo with us but not a Google Home, so we had to run out to the store to buy a Google Home to demo our product on it. Second, all of our demo-ware runs on Wi-Fi, and guess what—they didn't have Wi-Fi in the building. We had to use someone's hot spot from their personal phone account to connect our demos.

We were the last company of the four to present. A cofounder and I were sitting in the meeting room, waiting for all these managing directors to come in after seeing the other presentations. We knew that each of these guys had the ability to sign off on a multimillion-dollar deal. We had a presentation of about thirty slides, all standard sales stuff, ready to show. Was it going to be enough?

When they all streamed in, I immediately noticed they all looked totally exhausted. And here we were about to show them more slides. I turned to my cofounder and said, "You know what? Let's switch things up." Switching things up is my MO. Rarely do I stick to plans; I intuitively go with what I feel is right. "Let's just do five minutes of introductions," I said, "and then let's play with the technology for the rest of the meeting. These guys need a break. Let's give them something a little different."

And that's exactly what we did. We told them who we were, our background in academia, and what made us different. Then, for the next fifty-five minutes, we let them play with our demos—and they were completely engaged. Because the thing about Clinc is that when you actually experience it, it's like nothing you've ever seen before.

I was playing with all of the demos across all of the platforms, from a phone to Alexa to Google Home, showing how you could have the same conversation with each one. I showed them how we had their Pubclays logo on it. I said, "Check out this platform. It allows you to build any experience you want," and then I adjusted the experience right in front of them and showed them how it automatically updated across all the platforms. I had the panel give me questions to ask the AI, specific questions we couldn't have anticipated or preprogrammed.

In the audience were two people: Gilda Johnson and her boss,

Rahim. During that demo, they became true believers. Gilda said it was the best AI experience she'd ever had. "I don't care if you're a start-up," she said. "I don't care that you're in America. You guys can build the best experience." She became our champion in that meeting, and after the meeting, we were selected as Publays' AI vendor moving forward.

After that demonstration, IPsoft was completely out. Clinc was in. And that was just the start of our journey with Publays.

When we started working with them, the first thing they did was hand us a spec originally derived from the IPsoft spec of what to build. "Okay, Clinc," they said, "as a starting point, build this."

We knew the spec was no good—but also, they had just paid us a ton of money, so we did as they asked. And I hated the experience every step of the way. I knew it was not a good manifestation of what our technology could do. When Gilda came to visit us in Ann Arbor, I said, "Gilda, I wouldn't put my name on that experience."

"What?" she said. "Then why did you build it? I don't want an experience you wouldn't put your name on."

"Wait," I said, "you didn't know that we were given this spec? I assumed everybody knew that's what they were asking me to do." So, we threw out the spec and rebuilt it the Clinc way, and the results were off the chart.

We've got to do things the Clinc way.

I dealt with the same issue with "Mells Garbo," a big US bank, when I had to build something I didn't want to put my name on. We almost did it with "America Bank," but we had a customer summit that America Bank came to, and Gilda told everybody this story. Now America Bank loves what we're building for them. One of the leaders was so excited about it, he wanted to demo it to me. I was like, "Dude, you realize I'm the one who built it." It was awesome.

When we did things the Clinc way, Pubclays got equally excited. The first place Pubclays deployed our conversational AI was in Facebook Messenger. There, our conversational AI guided consumers in how to handle challenges like fraud issues, where twenty million people had access to our technology through the Pubclays deployments.

DELIVER AT ALL COSTS FOR PUBCLAYS

In our journey with Pubclays, there have been many interesting challenges. One day, Gilda called me and yelled for forty-five minutes—which is a great sign. It's a great sign because it means you have a relationship with the folks on this mission with you that's so close and intimate, they aren't afraid to yell at you. When you don't have a close relationship, you'll usually just get dropped with some weird, vague excuse like, "We've decided to go in another direction." But because we were on a mission together, Pubclays didn't do that. Instead, our key point person called and yelled at me, which enabled us to fix the problem and continue working together on our mission.

In this case, the issue was with our product delivery timeline for Pubclays working with their development team in India. "Jason, this is embarrassing," Gilda said. "My boss says it's not up and running right now. Our teams haven't been able to deploy your stack in Pune. You're not delivering on your promise."

I said, "Gilda, this is the first I'm hearing of this. Let me get on it right away, and I will call you back tomorrow."

Immediately, I deployed resources. By the next day, I had two of my top people on flights to India—and this was when we were still small and cash sensitive. But we had to do what had to be done. We had to deliver on our promise.

When our engineers arrived in India, they were shocked by what they found. They described it as basically a sweatshop for engineers. These engineers get paid a measly $10,000 a year to sit elbow to elbow at tiny tables and form an engineering assembly line. One guy was responsible for downloading the software. Then he passed it to the guy next to him, who was responsible for unzipping the software. Next to him was a guy responsible for putting it into the right folders. This description may be a simplification, but it's not very far from the truth.

We didn't know anything about the working model in this Indian office. We had no experience working with this type of engineering or assembly-line process. We expected that they would be engineers working like we did. Not only was it an odd working model for engineers, but our future-grade tech was beyond their capabilities. We didn't even know this kind of approach to engineering teams existed in the world. And now we could understand why there were so many challenges, why they needed our help.

The leaders in India were also very political, so they liked to blame the vendor. They knew they weren't producing the best product, and they were very anxious about it, so they were always trying to find someone else to blame. When their hirer was Pubclays, it was very easy to blame the little start-up American vendor.

Our engineers spent two weeks in India, got the deployment done, and built a deep understanding of the dynamics of the company. Gilda was thrilled and even flew to Ann Arbor to visit and celebrate with us.

Now, let's compare this to working with a company like Nuance or IPsoft. We mobilized resources to get things done. We went to India when we needed to. We went to London when we needed to. We were on a mission together, and we took care of the people we were on a mission with. With a big company like IPsoft, everything has to go through a bureaucracy. If there's an issue that needs to be fixed or if you ask for a feature customization, you have to put in a ticket, and it takes six or seven months to accomplish.

> Our greatest success occurs when our missions are aligned with those we serve.

This is how big businesses work—and it's why they don't succeed. We vowed never to work that way. This stuff is so difficult to get right. You have to be nimble and scrappy in order to get anything done and keep everything working. You need to be able to have someone call you, yell at you for forty-five minutes, then get solutions the next day.

One of the things I focus on with my salespeople is making sure they have real relationships with people. Our greatest success occurs when our missions are aligned with those we serve. We want everyone involved, in our company and in our customers' companies, to deeply care about what we're doing and the product we're bringing to market. We want to work with people who want to see this next generation of technological awesomeness happen and see it improve the lives of their customers.

That's what people like Gilda care about, and it's why even though we start as professional colleagues, we ultimately become partners and friends. Together we are focused and aligned in our vision.

CHAPTER 8

ENDLESS POSSIBILITIES

The conversational AI revolution has only just begun. Every industry wants in—and it's easy to see why. Think about it: AI doesn't get annoyed with you bothering it. AI doesn't eat, doesn't sleep. It's always there, always ready to help. It's a lot to ask of a living, breathing human being—to always be readily available to talk to you. Conversational AI gives enterprises an opportunity to have assistance always there and immediately accessible.

Plus, on the business side, there are massive cost savings. You can replace the human cashier at a fast-food restaurant with a voice ordering assistant. You can have AI in your call center answering questions all day and night. You can have an AI take notes for you and automatically highlight the important content.

It also makes the experience more consistent and predictable. Take a fast-food restaurant, for example. The drive-through attendant is supposed to upsell. If the consumer says, "I want a cheeseburger and a Coke," the attendant is supposed to say, "Do you want to add fries and make a meal out of that?" However, the compliance rates for upselling are extremely low. Why? Because humans don't consistently do it. As a business, you want things done consistently while still being adaptable to the individual consumer's needs. That's what true conversational AI can do.

Another advantage of AI is not just the user interface, but access to knowledge. If I asked a bank representative to tell me how much I spent at restaurants on the last vacation I took, they wouldn't have immediate access to that information—and chances are they wouldn't find it out for me because it's way too much work. And if I say, "Compare that to the vacation before," forget about it. No way would that person go back through every transaction, find the right dates, look for restaurants, add it all up, and do a comparison.

With an AI that is connected to your bank account, you can ask, "How much did I spend in Orlando last week at restaurants?" And the AI can immediately calculate it and even show you which restaurants in a pie chart. All that information and knowledge is readily and instantly available. These are the kinds of things that are possible with virtual assistants that are not so easy with humans.

How does this interconnection actually work? It's similar to a mobile app. The app on your phone is connected to your bank account on the bank's server. It's an interface to access that information, which the server provides. Now, imagine replacing that mobile app with a virtual assistant that can engage in conversation.

Usually, companies will buy the virtual assistant platform, which allows them to train the AI to understand the human language necessary for its task. Once it understands human language, you can plug it into data using application programming interfaces, or APIs. Basically, messages are sent from the virtual assistant to the business logic code, and then the business logic code can provide information through the API back to the virtual assistant, which then generates the response back to the user. This way, you hook the business interfaces that have the data right into the virtual assistant platform to create that modality of accessing information for the consumer.

In other words, the business is connected to Clinc's brain. The data comes from the business. The brain, the thinking, is happening in Clinc's cloud with our deployment model. And the experience is being had at the endpoint, in the consumer's interaction with the device connected to that cloud.

We can take one trained AI, one trained brain, and simultaneously plug it into Alexa, a mobile phone app, Facebook Messenger, a TV that has a microphone in it, a drive-through kiosk, or something else. You can plug the brain into any of these endpoints that have the ability to "speak."

Clinc is just at the beginning of its journey—and we are growing exponentially. We made our first deployment at the end of 2018. As of this writing, more than thirty-one million people use our tech, and we are on a trajectory to rapidly grow to close to a hundred million across multiple use cases and deployments.

The stories I could tell you about all our use cases and deployments are nearly endless. You've heard some of them already, and while I can't possibly tell them all, I'll share a few more to show you just how many different ways conversational AI can be used.

BANKING

Our banking successes aren't limited to Europe and America. In late 2017, we launched to six million Isbank users in Turkey. Since then, the week-to-week usage of our virtual assistant has risen. We have millions of people using it every week, and the number of queries is increasing over time. In other words, our virtual assistant is gaining traction in Turkey as we speak.

We were expecting the virtual assistant to be hyped up in the beginning, then slowly taper off into some sustained level of usage. That's what typically happens with conversational AI. Siri tapered off. Alexa tapered off. Instead, our virtual assistant is getting more and more popular because it has such sticky use cases.

As soon as you use our financial assistant, you can tell that it's different. You don't have to say specific phrases worded a specific way to get it to execute a command. You can have a real conversation. It keeps track as you talk of what's going on. If you refer back to something you said earlier, it remembers. If you make a mistake and correct yourself, it will correct that information.

For example, transferring money is so easy with voice. You don't have to tap seventeen times on your phone to do it. You can just say, "Send five hundred bucks to Mom," and it'll work. You could say, "Drop five hundred bones in Mom's account," and that will work too. You don't have to say it in a way that follows certain rules. You just have to communicate like a person, and it works.

FAST FOOD

I've shared a lot of stories about how we've brought AI into the banking industry. But our AI has gone far beyond that—sometimes into places I never expected or intended.

The reason we got into QSR (quick-service restaurants) is that a popular fast-food restaurant I'll call Mac Ronald's reached out to us. When Clinc started out, a company called MindMeld was one of the top conversational AI companies. It's now been acquired by Cisco, but back then it was an independent company. Apparently, one of the MindMeld people went to work for Mac Ronald's, and then Mac

Ronald's started thinking about conversational AI. The MindMeld guy had heard of Clinc, and what's funny is he didn't recommend MindMeld to Mac Ronald's; instead, he said, "We should check out Clinc." And someone contacted us.

This was before I even knew we would go outside financial services—but I had been talking for years about how frustrating it is when I order at Mac Ronald's and they get it wrong. Before we had kids, I always ordered the same thing: two cheeseburgers, a ten-piece nugget, no sauce, and a large diet Coke. And inevitably, they'd ask me to repeat my order or ask me what sauce I wanted.

I knew that conversational AI would solve this problem, so I decided for fun to try to build our AI for a drive-through. And then, coincidentally, Mac Ronald's reached out to us to build an AI for a drive-through. At this point I wasn't personally handling a lot of accounts, because I was starting to separate myself from sales, but I wanted to be involved with this one. It was important to me because Mac Ronald's was part of my life, and I wanted to experience my own work.

It was an innovation-lab-type group at Mac Ronald's that was trying to do this. Dennis, our head of sales at the time, had a call with them, and I told him, "You've got to get us on-site. People need to see, touch, and feel this experience. If you can get me on-site, I'll sanction the build-out of the demo."

Dennis secured us an on-site visit, and our engineer Parker had the demo built in two days. It's the same demo we now use for another customer of ours, "Turk-Fil-A." It's like a blank-slate human brain you can train with new data sets and let it learn new capabilities.

This totally perplexes our investors. Other companies use the old rules-based approaches. Anytime they want to add a new capability or fix any issue, it's a huge, laborious process. It makes scalability nearly impossible. Because our models learn entirely from data sets, once those data sets are collected and curated the right way, it learns the right stuff to be able to understand anything. So, we have it read the whole Turk-Fil-A menu, and then it knows everything on the menu.

Once it knows the menu, we need it to be able to understand all the ways people might order. The way we train those experiences is through crowdsourcing. We launch a job where we ask ten thousand people to order their favorite food, from Mac Ronald's or any restaurant. That gives us a broad sample of how people go about ordering their food, and that's the data we use to train that capability. The way our technology works, if you get good data, all you have to do is push a button, and you'll get a phenomenal experience.

I showed Mac Ronald's the demo in another RFP. As soon as they experienced it, they made us an incredible offer. But there was one problem: it came with an exclusivity clause. They wanted us to agree not to work with any other presence in the market.

"You're going to have to relax that clause," I said.

"We're Mac Ronald's," they said. "We need that clause. That's our culture."

"Well, in that case," I said, "hear you; no." I was not going to sign away all that potential business. If you ask Lingjia, she'd probably say we should have gone for it. But then we wouldn't have been able to do any other activity in the QSR world. That's a lot to commit to for a one-time project. What if they never even took it into production? That was certainly a possibility.

So, even though we won the relationship initially, we actually ended up saying no to Mac Ronald's. And now we're working with a number of other QSRs. In fact, literally all of our QSRs have been inbound, meaning they've come to us. We've had a number of projects with Turk-Fil-A. Industry magazines like *QSR* and *The Spoon* love to cover us, because no one else is doing this in the restaurant space. Why? Because it's way too hard. We're able to do it because we've built technology that can create these crazy robust experiences in no time, as long as they are provided with enough data.

Within all these QSRs, there are many parts of the organization. There are the mobile-app people, the drive-through people, and the counter-service people. And they're all interested in implementing our AI.

I couldn't be more excited. QSR is something that touches every American. Everybody gets fast food sometimes, so it's an area where I know our technology can touch countless lives.

GAMING

Just as QSR was not on our radar, Clinc had no plan to get into gaming. Even though I loved video games as a kid, and still do, I'd never even thought of it.

One day, I was checking in with one of our engineers, Connor. He was an intern I'd taken a special interest in because of his extraordinary talent. He's one of those guys who builds difficult stuff just for fun, and anyone who challenges themselves for fun is someone I like to work with. It's almost a guaranteed way into Clinc.

> Anyone who challenges themselves for fun is someone I like to work with.

"Hey, Connor, how are you doing?" I asked.

"I'm good," he said. "Working on some cool stuff. I made this thing with the Clinc stack."

"What thing?" I asked.

"I'm using the Unity [video game creation] engine, and then I integrated it with this thing. Now you can use conversational AI to control a drone in this game."

I had no idea he was working on something like this. He brought his laptop over and showed me how he could control this drone in the game by saying, "Change your lights to blue" or "Go ten feet over there."

"Hell, yeah!" I exclaimed. "Let's build this out and launch a go-to-market at GDC." GDC is the Game Developer's Conference, the largest conference of its kind, and it was happening in March. Gaming wasn't something the company had ever planned on doing, but what Connor had built was so cool, I made the decision then and there to develop it. It felt completely aligned with our work.

In addition, I had a personal connection: gaming is where I first started experimenting with AI when I was a teenager. When I was fifteen, I created a program I called the Quake Random Map Generator (QRMG), which used artificial intelligence to build new levels in the game Quake. Essentially, it was an AI-level designer. Soon, thousands of players were using this program I created.

As soon as I created QRMG, I knew I wanted to generalize it so it could work on other games. So, when I started college, I began working on URGE: the Universal Random Generation Engine. This program could randomly generate levels for any game. I released it for four or so games and changed its name to Erbium.

Beyond QRMG, URGE/Erbium introduced a special programming language to describe the construction of three-dimensional geometries. You can articulate code in procedural, programmatic ways that are Turing complete, meaning it can simulate the algorithm's logic—and that's a novelty. There are published papers about non-Turing complete approaches to do this, but Erbium being Turing complete means it's as powerful as any programming language in existence for 3D geometrical features. It's a contribution that literally no one else on the planet is working on, at least as far as I'm aware.

Unfortunately, Professor Soffa wasn't as into gaming as I was. In fact, she saw it as a distraction. "Jason, you have to focus," she would say. "Stop talking to me about video games." So, as I started my PhD and got caught up in the world of academia, I had to abandon Erbium. But it's a passion project and one that I will absolutely return to and finish before I die, because nothing like it exists in the world. There are no games in which the levels are generated by an AI. Even though I started it when I was fifteen, it's still a new invention.

With this backstory, I was psyched to be bringing something to GDC, which is well known in the gaming industry. GDC is cool because it's not a consumer conference. It's exclusively for technical people, business owners, people working on these products. The demo we launched at GDC is a scene with a shopkeeper who sells weapons. You can ask the shopkeeper what he has in stock, look over his selection, find a specific weapon, narrow things down by category or power or enchantment, buy weapons, sell things you have in your inventory—all through normal conversation.

At GDC, I invited a random person from the audience to come onstage in front of the crowd and talk to the shopkeeper demo. That can be a risky move for any company, because you can't control what the person is going to do or say.

The guy came onstage, clearly skeptical, and started to interact with the shopkeeper. I let him go for a few minutes before I said, "Thanks, man—that was awesome." But the guy was so enthralled by the experience that he wanted to keep playing with it. So we let him ask a few more things.

It was exactly the experience you want your gamers to have: the interaction is so engaging they want to keep going. It didn't require any training or priming. There was no manual he had to read, no language he had to learn, no commands he had to memorize. There wasn't a list of four questions he could pick from. He could ask anything he wanted, in any way he wanted, and the shopkeeper could understand and respond. You can interact with it completely intuitively. And we built it in one week with one engineer.

After GDC, the interest flowed in. We started talking with Epic, Sony, Unity, Naughty Dog, Fortnite, and Far Cry, and now we're moving forward with a number of them.

For example, we've collaborated with Unity to use conversational AI to build content. In other words, conversational AI game designers can use speech to actually build the game. This reduces the level of technical requirement to get started with game design. Say you're building a level of a game. Instead of needing to know all the coding or having to learn the whole platform or having to manually program everything, you can say, "Hey, I want a chair over there, and put a tank over there, and let's make this room ten by ten." You don't have to manipulate this crazy interface. You can just articulate what you want the environment to be, and it will be created in real time. We've been working with Unity to build this experience, and it may become a standard part of their platform. And I can tell you—it'll be a game changer.

AUTOMOTIVE

We're not just changing the game for game designers and gamers; we're also changing the game for auto designers and drivers. In fact, Ford became interested in our work from an academic research standpoint before we even started the company. After our work on Sirius and Lucida, which received a fair amount of press coverage, one of Ford's senior researchers emailed me. "I saw this article about your research," he said. "I'd love to meet and chat with you about how we can work together." Ford then engaged our research lab on a project called ADASA, putting conversational AI in the vehicle, about which we ultimately published top-tier papers together.

When Ford issued us a $250,000 grant to conduct research together, they gave us a prototype car and said, "As a research project, put conversational AI in this car." The way research grants like this work, the grant is basically funding PhD students. You can take that money and do research around a problem of common interest between the lab and funding company. For the sake of the relationship, you hope the outcome of the research and publications are aligned with the interests of the grant giver, but they are not required to be, and it's the scientific duty of the lab to pursue truth over all else.

Ultimately, the first Ford grant led to an incredibly successful research paper, and it has also had a massive impact on Ford. Though I can share the research work my university lab did with Ford, I'm not allowed to disclose whether Clinc has provided solutions for Ford. What I can say is our research relationship has had a major impact on the company and on a specific employee there too. He received a couple of promotions because of his work with us.

Initially, when we approached the automotive market with Clinc's technology, we showed them the financial services demo we had created so they could see the conversational capabilities of the technology. Unfortunately, that community didn't have the ability to visualize replacing financial intelligence with automotive AI. When they saw the conversational AI for financial services, they said, "Okay, but that's for financial services. That can't work in a car. I don't think we can spend our money on this." I was frustrated, because the core technology can be trained in any domain, but they couldn't see that.

So, I had Parker put together an automotive demo, again in about two days. We recorded a video of it and sent it to decision makers who were not sold by the financial services demo.

The next day, they called us. They were all in.

HEALTHCARE AND MEDICAL

Conversational AI isn't confined to the consumer experience. It can also make the internal processes of an organization much faster and more efficient, which is especially exciting in the healthcare and medical fields.

One of our medical use cases was with a major healthcare technology provider we'll call Hytter. Hytter provides medical devices to essentially the entire medical industry, and they had a big initiative to do a digital transformation and provide apps to the industry. One of the domains they were especially interested in was stroke identification. When someone falls over or has some kind of an emergency, it's incredibly important to be able to rapidly identify whether it's a stroke.

Typically, EMTs will do a systematic stroke assessment in the ambulance that includes twelve signs to look for to establish whether or not the person is having a stroke. As you can imagine, the environment inside an ambulance is not a quiet one. There's a lot of commotion as they try to administer care while transporting the patient to the hospital. Then, when they get to the hospital, they have to transfer their assessment to a doctor, who has to determine what is going on. It's a very inefficient system.

We realized this would be a perfect opportunity for conversational AI. As a medical-care provider, you may not be able to take notes during your assessment of the patient because you are focused on physically doing the assessment, meaning your hands aren't free. If you have AI there listening, it can accumulate that information for you, creating better outcomes for patients and likely saving lives.

We knew the challenge would be that the AI would have to be able to understand the messy language of people talking in a hectic environment. In order to pull the correct data for the stroke assessment, the AI would need to be able to pick out the relevant and nonrelevant things the EMT and patient are saying and do it unobtrusively. The EMT couldn't be dealing with an app in their hand, trying to push a button to record the information. The AI would need to passively be in the environment listening to what's going on and complete the twelve-point assessment from the commotion of interactions.

The EMT could be having a normal conversation with the patient: "How's your family? Can you follow my pen with your eyes? No? Okay." And the AI would pick up, "The patient couldn't follow the pen with their eyes." Then the EMT may say, "Move your left leg for me. Okay, the patient wasn't able to move his left leg," and amid all the chatter, the AI could pick up, "The patient wasn't able to move his left leg." While the EMT maintains a regular conversation with the patient to put them at ease, the AI is completing the twelve-point stroke assessment. It's always on, and it's always hands-free. It plucks the relevant bits of information without needing any extra input from the doctor.

Then, that information will be available digitally, and it can be sent to the doctor well before the patient gets to the hospital. When the ambulance arrives, the doctor won't have to read the EMT's assessment; they will already have it on their screen and be primed and prepared to take care of the patient.

This isn't just theoretical. We are deploying it as we speak. We have built out this digital experience and tested it, and now we're on the journey of piloting it with real EMTs and patients. It's a use case that uses technology beyond keyword matching to do complicated things that were not possible until we solved it. In fact, Hytter had failed pilots with Nuance and IPsoft—billion-dollar companies that are trying to operate in this space. When we deployed our tech, Hytter said, "We never imagined that it could work this well." They were so jaded by their bad experiences with other AI they could scarcely believe what they were seeing.

The nice thing about a use case like this is we're adding something that wasn't there before. This way of bringing virtual assistants into market helps people do their jobs better, and it does so safely. If the AI doesn't help, then the person continues to do their job as they previously did, no harm done. And if the AI does help, it might save someone's life.

We're also working on something similar with another start-up, Obex, which is working with a doctor at the Barrow Neurological Institute. The doctor is one of the top luminaries in neurosurgery, and he created the AI based on the idea of saving himself and other doctors like him time in any way they could.

Obex has a platform on which patients can watch automated instructional videos so the doctor can focus on other things while the patient is getting the necessary information. The platform's other function is to record the whole doctor-patient session, audio and video. That recording can then be shared with the patient, so the patient can reference and remember what he and the doctor discussed.

Obex aims to get their solution into every doctor's office. By early 2020, they had already put it into about thirty-two hospitals, and the doctor from Barrow wanted to take it to the next level. I met with their CEO and showed him our tech, and he loved what he saw.

This is similar to something we're working on with Olive, a company that provides automation-like systems to about two hundred hospitals. One thing that takes up a huge amount of doctors' and nurses' time is record keeping. The extensive medical-record data entry is very time consuming for nurses and doctors. Right now, doctors will pay medical students and nurses a salary just to sit in meetings and take notes, specifically recording symptoms and patient responses. This costs a huge amount of money, and it wastes the valuable time of those students and nurses.

Clinc partnered with Olive to build a system in which the AI will hear doctors and nurses using natural, messy language and enter the relevant information into the system, automatically filling out forms as they talk with the patient. The AI will be able to complete about 80 percent of the form, saving the doctor or nurse the time and money it would take them or someone they've hired to do it manually. It also will enable them to spend more time with their patients.

These kinds of applications demonstrate the immense opportunities for conversational AI to improve healthcare. It can create a revolution in the healthcare space.

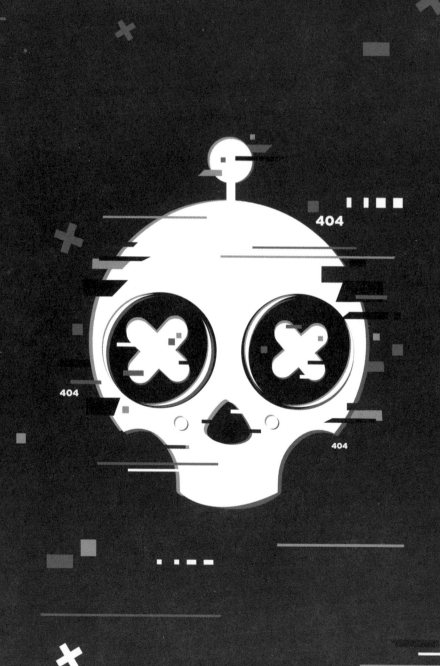

CHAPTER 9

THE FUTURE IS NOW

THERE'S SO MUCH MORE TO DO

Along with what I've already shared, Clinc has several more projects in the works. For example, we are working on training virtual assistants to decipher long, boring, technical manuals to save time and aggravation. What if you could take a manual, put it into an engine, and watch a virtual assistant that knows everything in that manual pop out? Then, instead of searching, you could just ask the assistant a question, and it would have an answer immediately. If I had a virtual assistant built into my TV, I could say, "Hey, TV, how do I fix the aspect ratio?" Or even better, I could say, "Hey, TV, fix the aspect ratio," and the virtual assistant would do it for me.

Technically, building a virtual assistant out of unstructured text that knows everything in that text is an extremely difficult problem. The Watson AI that played *Jeopardy* is an example of trying to do that. But the way that technology works, it's not a virtual assistant. It just answers questions. You can't actually talk to it.

In order to create a product-grade virtual assistant automatically, we have to relax some of the constraints. We have to move from unstructured understanding to virtual assistant. How can we turn up the dial on the amount of structure required so we can generate a good virtual assistant? Then, how do we get to a place where we can automate the amount of structure we need to inject into the manual?

This is a universally applicable idea, and it's just one of the things I'm pondering. We're spending a lot of time working on AI to help build AI: artificial intelligence that will assist you in building other good artificial intelligence.

THE DREAM GOES ON

Beyond what we've created at Clinc, I continue to examine the possibilities of where AI could go next.

I'd love to see conversational AI used in toys, in ways that can help kids learn and develop. I'd love to see conversational AI that can help people program and develop software. I'd love to see conversational AI for productivity. When I'm driving home, I can say, "Hey, dude, let me talk to you about my day and the stuff I need to do." I can then rattle off everything that needs my attention, from errands to appointments to emails, and the AI would organize my thoughts, create schedules, and make to-do lists. This is something we could build today and have ready to go in a couple of months—if we had the people and the time.

The frontier for conversational AI is endless and thrilling.

There is so much we could bring into existence that could change the world, but we have to be careful not to spread ourselves too thin. That's why I'm so excited for the AI world to continue expanding. That's why I'm so excited for you to join me on this journey.

The frontier for conversational AI is endless and thrilling, and I can't wait to see where we go next. I have so many ideas for future applications that I would love to see happen. Just in the process of writing this book, I've had so many new thoughts about how conversational AI can be used. There is so much to do, so much that can be done. And all we need to get there is you.

BE A PART OF THE AI REVOLUTION

Artificial intelligence has the opportunity to make people more efficient and productive; the places it can be applied are endless. But you have to think it through. Don't do conversational AI for conversational AI's sake. You have to know in your heart that you're making things better. It should be something you would want to use yourself. You have to be your first user, and if it's actually improving your life, then you know you're doing it right.

The only way to do that is to tinker and try things, and there's a wide spectrum of options available. Don't go for technology that isn't the best. If you're using a technology that only allows you to build superscripted, superlimited interactions that require a manual, you're doing it wrong.

There are a lot of folks trying to figure out how to evaluate conversational AI. For me, the only metric to consider is whether or not it's delivering on the promise of what it needs to do. And the only way to determine that is to try it yourself. Are users engaged? Are they coming back? Are they completing what you want them to complete using that conversational AI? Those are the metrics to evaluate whether or not the AI is working.

A lot of people think the best metric for measuring AI is accuracy. The problem is the methodology for measuring accuracy isn't accurate. The methodology often used to generate accuracy scores is a training and a testing set. They have a pool of data they use for training, and they'll test a random selection of that data. However, the tested data is randomly selected from the training data set, meaning the AI is uniformly trained on that data. So, of course, the results are always good. The test will show 98 percent accuracy. But then they launch the AI, and when it interacts with actual users, it works only 2 percent of the time.

You can't use those kinds of metrics when you're evaluating conversational AI. You have to use the metrics of how it performs when it's actually being used. How many times did the virtual assistant solve the problem? How many times did the person have to talk to a human agent? Engagement is also an important metric. Are people coming back to interact with this AI?

I advocate what I call the gut test. Just use it. Play with it. Play with it as if it's a human in the room. Talk to it naturally. If it's working for you, it's in a good place. Often, people will launch virtual assistants that don't pass the gut test. You have to try something out to make sure it works.

GETTING TO PRODUCTION

Many companies make claims they can't back up. They will say, "We have all this research." But the research won't actually be in the product. You have to see it, touch it, and feel it yourself to really know. *You* have to make sure it works.

Unfortunately, a lot of companies will process themselves out.

For example, they may create a spec sheet with boxes that need to be checked, followed by a user study in which people complete certain tasks and check off those boxes. If those boxes are checked, the company will say, "Great. Go to market." But they never use the product themselves, an absolute must if you are going to be on the forefront of tech. There is no replacement for intuition, for that gut check.

For an enterprise, this starts with a POC, or proof of concept. This means having the vendor build out the experience and deploy it for you to play with. We'll run those for thirty to fifty days. The next phase is the gut check. Is the experience as advertised? If it is, you can move into the pilot phase, which usually lasts about six months. During that phase, the product is launched to a limited number of users. That number could be ten thousand, thirty thousand, or three hundred thousand, depending on the size of your company. Then, you watch how it performs in the market. If it performs well, you can launch it to all your users.

This is the process we're following with America Bank. The innovation labs at these banks tinker with stuff, try stuff out for about a year, and then some of it will make it over to the business units and go into production.

We started working with America Bank's innovation lab in that first POC stage. It was a thirty-day POC in which we took our financial virtual assistant and deployed it to two hundred internal employees across the bank, integrating it into their actual data. Those two hundred employees can now use our financial genie to ask about their finances, their spending, where the nearest ATM is, and anything else they need.

Five days into its launch, all two hundred people were playing with this thing. On day five, we received an email from the business unit saying, "We'd like to take you to production by Labor Day." They had tried plenty of other products, including Nuance's Nina and their own system built in-house, but none of it passed the gut check. Then they tried Clinc, gut checked it, and went with it.

This is what you want to do with any AI vendor you're considering. You want to actually get the product and give it a solid test run to see if it works. You need to be an actual user. That's the key. Mark Zuckerberg started Facebook because it was something he wanted for himself. He was a user. Same thing with Google, Twitter, and Airbnb. The guy who created Patagonia was a hiker who couldn't get the kind of hiking gear he wanted, so he created a company to make it.

CHALLENGE THE STATUS QUO

If you care about technology and improving quality of life for others, the best thing we can do with our organizations and companies is understand how we can apply these technologies to reduce costs and improve the customer experience.

If you're a consumer, I have one challenge for you: don't tolerate crap. Let the market know that you're picky, that you'll accept only the best. Only go with experiences that work for you, that work in your life. Don't allow companies and businesses to get away with cutting corners. Don't let them keep you ten years in the past. Be vocal. Hold companies accountable to using the best stuff out there. Make a change. The AI experience doesn't have to be negative. An amazing AI experience is possible. Don't give up on it.

And if you're a coder like me, I'll tell you what my fifteen-year-old self wrote to the people who visited my QRMG website: "To all the passionate programmers out there (Koder For Life Baby). Don't ever stop koding and learning."

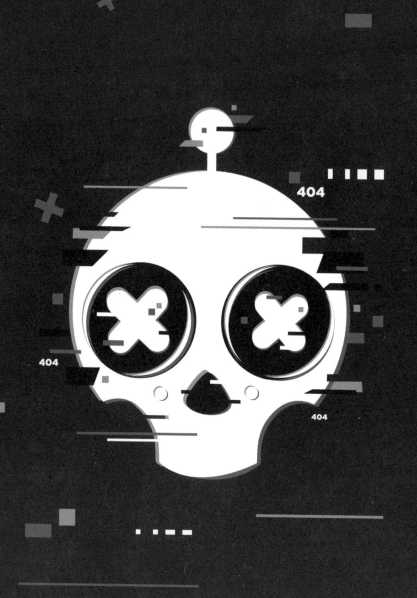

THE FUTURE IS OURS

When the *Enterprise*'s shipboard computer spoke in 1966, it was an exotic impossibility, and yet we envisioned it—and it took us only fifty years to start doing it well enough to be compelling. Now we're at the point of passing compelling and moving into a new era of conversational AI.

So, what could AI be if we overcome the conversational hump?

The way we experience this as consumers is through gradually more complex products. Right now, we have products that can play music, turn on lights, and look up the weather. That's interesting. Maybe next we're going to have a product that allows us to describe something we want to buy from Amazon, including all the details—color, shape, size, price range. The product will need the ability to follow multiple conversational turns. To make that experience as frictionless as possible, the AI needs to be able to draw from intuition. It needs to be able to reason out what product you want. Now, that's more interesting than just being able to turn on your lights.

You'll have agents able to negotiate and reason and solve problems as capably as a human being. Maybe there will be a product that allows you to negotiate a price for your nanny (something relative to my life these days). That would require the AI to use my history of knowledge and references, as well as have the ability to negotiate and reason.

We'll also see a larger range of interactions with the environment around us. Say I'm having a Zoom meeting. Instead of clicking on the link, waiting for the Zoom call to open, making sure the host is recording the meeting, and finally getting the meeting going, I could say, "Hey, drop me into that Zoom call I'm supposed to have. Also, make sure Kendra starts the recording. Is she around?"

"Kendra's walking to her desk," the AI could say, as it opens up the Zoom meeting on my computer. "She has her phone, so I'll remind her to start the recording." By the time I sit down at my computer for the meeting, everything is good to go.

As we see these gradual increases in capability, we'll start seeing a ubiquity of these products. What might that ubiquity look like in your life in concrete terms?

The first thing will be virtual assistants everywhere—your house, phone, car, every store you visit. What does that look like? Imagine you're in your house and you ask, "Hey, do we have any eggs?"

"You have four eggs left," your assistant replies.

"Remind me to get those on my way home," you say. You've got to go to Best Buy, so you figure you'll pick up the eggs while you're out.

You hop in your car and say, "Get me directions to Best Buy." The navigation comes up, and your assistant tells you that you don't have enough gas to get there. "Let's stop at whatever the closest gas station with the best price is," you say, and your car GPS automatically updates the navigation.

After getting gas, you head to Best Buy. Your kid is set on getting this hot new game that just came out for Christmas. You get to the store and ask the kiosk at the entrance where the toy is. "Aisle 4," says the AI kiosk. "We have three in stock, but two other people just asked about it, so there is likely only one left." You head to aisle 4 and grab the toy. As you walk out, you don't stop at checkout; the AI kiosk automatically scans the item and charges your credit card.

As you hop back in the car, the virtual assistant says, "Don't forget you need eggs. Would you like to go to your regular grocery store or the one on the way home?"

"The one on the way home," you say, and the GPS automatically pulls up the navigation to the grocery store most in line with your route home.

You get home and find your kid working on his math homework with the virtual assistant, giving you the time to cook a dinner for your whole family to sit down to together.

None of this is that far away. Amazon and Whole Foods are already prototyping automatic checkouts. At Clinc, we're building a math tutor that walks kids through math problems piece by piece. We're already in the early stages; we're starting to see virtual assistants everywhere, and we're seeing them get more complex.

Right now, there are different virtual assistants for different things. Ultimately, they could all be one. There's nothing technologically preventing us from building a capability where all these experiences are handled by the same virtual assistant who is with you all the time.

Imagine being able to find out from your assistant whether Best

Right now, there are different virtual assistants for different things. Ultimately, they could all be one.

Buy has the toy and how many are in stock before you even get in the car. Imagine that it can even reserve one for you to pick up that afternoon, maybe even prepay for it so you can just walk into the store and get it.

That assistant can manage your house and car. It can interact with stores and your travel plans. Maybe it's in a headset or in a small ear pod so it can be with you all the time, like our phones are now. It can learn about you, get to know you, maybe have personality profiles to match your mood. Maybe that one assistant will even have a name and a personality, like Tony Stark's J.A.R.V.I.S. in the *Iron Man* movies.

In an ideal world, all of this would be interconnected into one system. You could say, "Hey, Alexa, I need to open up an account. My name's Bob Jones. Oh yeah, I guess you need my address too. It's 123 Elm Street in San Antonio, Texas. Let's see; what else do you need?" And you can continue in that messy, conversational way. With Clinc's brain, Alexa would be able to interpret and understand all of that. As it is, Alexa's own brain, Lex, can't follow that way of speaking. (We actually have a partnership with Alexa to put our brain behind Amazon Connect.)

Unfortunately, interconnectivity is one of the massive barriers to this kind of all-purpose virtual assistant. Everything isn't connected. Your bank can't communicate directly with the store, which can't communicate directly with your virtual assistant.

That barrier can be transcended in only one of two ways: cooperation or monopoly. As humans, we tend to resist both of those things. We rise up against monopolies, and we resist cooperation. Technology can't solve that problem; overcoming that barrier is something humans are going to have to solve on their own.

Will these developments change the way we interact with each other and with the world? Of course. Habits are already changing. In China, nobody texts by hand anymore. Everybody uses voice texting.

But our human interactions are constantly being jacked up by technology. We used to write letters. Then we wrote emails. Now we can text or instant message or Snapchat in the blink of an eye. Dating has changed drastically thanks to dating apps; it's hardly recognizable to people just a microgeneration older. If I had to date today, I'd have no idea what to do! And yet the folks who have only experienced it the current way usually think, "Oh man, life must have sucked back then before dating apps. How did you do it?"

When the way we interact changes, it always bothers us. When we stopped writing letters and started sending emails, the older generation lamented, "The art of letter writing is dead! It's destroying our society as we know it!" Meanwhile, the generation that grew up with email is saying, "You have to wait two weeks for a letter to arrive, and then the response takes another two weeks—why would you ever want that?"

Only in the transition does it seem like a bad thing. Once we embrace it, we see how much easier and less complex it makes our everyday lives.

The frontier of what will work in society starts with the intelligence understanding us and our ability to interact with that intelligence. That's where we are now. Every year it's going to get more sophisticated, and as you increase the depth of sophistication, you'll get a breadth of ability to interact.

Once that happens, there are countless other frontiers to explore. There's creating the intelligence, and then there's the way we integrate that intelligence into ourselves. We have smartwatches that measure our heart rate. We have wireless earbuds connected to our phones. But there hasn't been much innovation beyond that. The market isn't producing more innovative ways to integrate AI into ourselves.

There's also the question of what the next step is beyond speech. The minimum complexity we're at now is not having to use an intermediary like a mouse, keyboard, or touch screen to interact. Those are intermediaries to the natural, evolved human way of interacting with each other, which is direct communication—that is, speech.

Instant gratification with minimal work drives us. You can speak something, and it will come into being. I could say, "I want a burger," and my virtual assistant would know my favorite burger place and my regular burger order. It could communicate that with the restaurant, order my burger, and have it arrive at my door. All I would have to do is say, "I want a burger."

But what's the next step? It's not too difficult to imagine that soon we won't even have to speak aloud; we'll be able to just think something, and the AI will do it. That could be a reality within a few generations—or less. There are already researchers working on how to transfer information directly from brain to brain, communicating purely via brain waves.

Then there's the realm of making AI not just human smart, but humanlike. Intelligence is interacting with others. So, you have to start by making that interaction smart, and then you can build upon it with other kinds of intelligences, like emotional intelligence. Once we solve the problem of the intelligence understanding us, of making it human smart, we can focus on the space of making AI more humanlike—with distinct personalities, even capable of empathy. There's already a lot of work being done on making the voices of conversational AI sound more like humans and less like robots.

What is exciting about all of this is that it's going to happen quicker than most people think. At Clinc, we're constantly astounded by what's possible as we're inventing along the way. As we continue to expand, we'll get to a place where the ease of interacting with machines and data becomes equivalent to the ease of interacting with human beings. At the rate AI is developing, I'd say we're about five to ten years away from being able to talk to AI as freely as if it were a human in the room.

And then where will we go? Is it so crazy for us to envision putting our consciousness into a computer? We're transcending animals by being able to actualize our wishes through technology. Considering how exponentially the rate of progress has been accelerating, I believe anything is possible.

It doesn't matter if you're a business owner, an employee, an engineer, or a person who simply thinks AI is insanely cool. We are on this crazy journey together, and anyone can do something big. Get out there and explore. Now is the moment. You can spend your time on something that will advance us as a civilization. There's no barrier to entry. So much information and education is available, ripe for the taking. Building this world is a community effort. We as a society need to think about how we move the needle forward to create that future. And everybody has a role in it. The future is always in front of us—so jump in!

ABOUT THE AUTHOR

Jason Mars's work is at the intersection of science, technology, and creativity. Jason's mission to have meaningful impact in the lives of every human is demonstrated by a long list of intellectual and technical contributions.

Jason is a professor of computer science at the University of Michigan, where he directs Clarity Lab, one of the best places in the world to be trained in topics spanning artificial intelligence, large-scale computing, and programming languages. Among numerous contributions, his lab pioneered award-winning work on Sirius (a.k.a. Lucida), the world's first open-source sophisticated virtual assistant that simultaneously hears, sees, and understands.

Jason Mars also founded Clinc, a record-breaking, cutting-edge AI company based in Ann Arbor, Michigan, where he led the development of the world's most advanced conversational AI. Focusing first on applying the technology in the banking industry, Clinc created a novel, customizable, voice-activated AI assistant and platform that connects humans with their financial stories. From there, Jason led the company's technology to address pressing challenges in the healthcare, automotive, and food-service industries. Under his technical vision and business leadership as CEO from 2015 to 2020, Clinc experienced substantial year-over-year growth, employing 120 employees, raising over $62 million in venture capital, and growing the business to around $10 million in annual recurring revenue with over seven million active users. In his service as CEO, he was named Bank Innovation's number two "Most Innovative CEO in Banking 2017" and number four in "Top 11 Technologists in Voice AI 2019."

Jason has devoted his career to solving difficult real-world problems, building some of the world's most sophisticated scalable systems for AI, computer vision, and natural language processing. This work has been recognized by Crain's Detroit Business's 2019 "40 under 40" for "career accomplishments, impact in their field, and contributions to their community." Prior to the University of Michigan, Jason was a professor at University of California San Diego, where he made a number of key contributions in cloud computing. He also worked at Google and Intel.

Jason's work constructing large-scale AI and deep-learning-based systems and technology has been recognized globally and continues to have a significant impact on industry and academia. Jason holds a PhD in computer science from the University of Virginia.